It's Not Always
Smart to Be Pretty

Janie Torbich

IT'S NOT ALWAYS SMART TO BE PRETTY

B.O.Y. Publications, Inc.
c/o Author Copyrights
P.O. Box 262
Lowell, NC 28098
betonyourselfent.com

Paperback ISBN: 978-1-955605-81-6
Hardback ISBN: 978-1-955605-82-3

Cover and Interior Design: B.O.Y. Enterprises, Inc.

Printed in the United States.

Table of Contents

Acknowledgements

I would like to extend my deepest thanks to those who have been instrumental in this journey and who have made this book possible.

First and foremost, to my mom—words cannot fully capture the depth of my gratitude for you. From day one, you have been my most devoted cheerleader, always believing in me even when I doubted myself. Your unshakeable support and fierce love have been a beacon of hope and strength in my life. Your unwavering faith in me has not only lifted my spirits but has also ignited a burning desire within me to reach for heights I once thought were beyond my grasp. In my darkest moments, your belief in me has been a guiding star, lighting the way and filling my heart with hope. Thank you for being my rock, my inspiration, and my greatest supporter.

To my dad, you are an extraordinary example of faith and strength. Your relationship with God has shown me the true meaning of commitment and devotion. Thank you for being such a profound influence in my life and for teaching me the importance of living with purpose and integrity.

To my sister, I want to express my deepest gratitude for setting the bar so high. Your remarkable achievements and boundless wisdom has always been a beacon of inspiration for me. Far from feeling overshadowed, your success has been a driving force, encouraging me to strive for greatness and push beyond my own perceived limits. Your grace and generosity in never making me feel less than amazing have motivated me more than you could ever know.

To my older brother, your adventurous spirit and the joy you've brought into my life have been truly invaluable. You've not only kept my mind engaged but also helped me move past my insecurities about my intelligence. I am deeply grateful for all the ways you've helped me grow and thrive.

To my younger brother, thank you for always seeing the best in me. Your unwavering belief in my intelligence and pride in my achievements have been a constant source of motivation. I'm incredibly proud of the way you've turned your life around, and even more inspired by your desire to help others do the same. Your support has made all the difference.

To Aunt Donna, I want to express my heartfelt gratitude for all the thank-yous you never received. Your thoughtful gestures of love—through countless cards for Valentine's Day, St. Patrick's Day, Easter, Halloween, Christmas, and birthdays—have been a constant source of warmth and joy in my life. Each card has been a reminder of your unwavering presence and the deep love you have shown me over the years. Your kindness has touched my heart deeply, and I am so grateful for the special place you hold in my life. Thank you for every sweet note and for being a true beacon of love and care.

To my friend Carmen, you are forever my angel and a cherished part of my life. Your unwavering obedience to God and your selflessness in taking time out of your day to pray and care for others, including me, mean the world to me. Your presence and support are a true blessing, and I am deeply grateful for everything you do. Your trustworthiness and authenticity shine through in all you do. My daughter Sadie Jane's life is a testament to your obedience to God, and for that, I am profoundly thankful.

To Matthew Pait and Kristen Pors from Pait Photography, thank you for capturing the most important part: the cover of my book. Even though they say, "don't judge a book by its cover," this cover will be judged, and you've made it so worthy of admiration. From the first time we met in 2019, when you took Daniel's and my engagement photos, you've always been so encouraging and patient. I love both of you so much. Your kindness and skill shone through, especially when you took Sadie's newborn pictures and our family photos. Thank you for always being willing to come anywhere to get the perfect shot.

To my book editor, Jamie King Jones, your patience and dedication have been extraordinary. When I first began this journey, my writing was a maze of run-on sentences and chaotic punctuation. Your guidance and hard work have transformed my words into a coherent and heartfelt narrative. I have learned so much from you, and your efforts have made a significant impact on this book.

I am immensely grateful for my publisher Otescia Johnson of B.O.Y. Enterprises for being the guiding light behind my book's publication. Before reaching out to you, I prayed for direction and clarity, and when we spoke, I felt an immediate and profound connection. Your voice and our conversation confirmed that you were the perfect choice to bring my book to life. I am proud and honored to have you as my publisher. Thank you for believing in my work and for your unwavering support.

To Jalyssa Lacy McRae at Studio J, I am deeply grateful for your exceptional talent in hair, makeup, and photography. Working with you has been a pleasure, and I'm proud to call you my friend. Your professionalism, creativity, and enthusiasm have made this journey enjoyable and successful. Your selflessness and willingness to help, especially with my girls and their pageant experience, have been truly appreciated. You've shown that beauty and brains go hand in hand, and for that, I am profoundly thankful.

To my sponsor my friend Jennifer, I am profoundly grateful for your guidance and support. You've helped me recognize and work on my character defects, and your insights have been invaluable in my personal growth. Thank you for being a constant source of wisdom and encouragement.

To my best friend Britt, thank you for our unstoppable and unbreakable friendship. Your support and understanding have been a constant in my life, and I am so grateful for the bond we share.

To Don I am the cream of the crop, and I miss you deeply. Your presence and influence have been a cherished part of my journey.

To my Coastal Finance team, Becky, Randy, and Joy: Becky, thank you for always believing in me and seeing beyond just my appearance. Your playful jokes about the number of flowers I've received, and my growing vase collection are always in good fun. I truly appreciate that you recognize my capabilities. Having you as my assistant manager is something I wouldn't trade for anything. We can finish each other's sentences and anticipate each other's moves without a word.

Randy, you are the best collections manager, and I'm so grateful to have you in this role. Your support is invaluable. Thank you for believing in me and always treating me with respect. You're our security guard, always protecting us and ensuring no one crosses boundaries. Your gentlemanly demeanor truly makes a world of difference.

Joy, it's been wonderful to see you grow in the 5 years you've worked for me. I'm thrilled that you're finding your stride.

Council, I'm deeply saddened that you're no longer here with us. If I could tell you one thing, it would be a heartfelt thank you. I'll always be your prettiest, and now, in your honor, I am shining as your brightest.

And to Jim and John, you both broke the mold for me. Thank you for believing in me and trusting me to become the person I am today.

To my wonderful Joy Elizabeth, thank you for your endless kindness and the inspiration you've provided. Your support during those late-night writing sessions and your thoughtful feedback has been invaluable. Continue to blaze your own trail with integrity and grace.

To my dear Riley, you have transformed my life in ways I never could have imagined. Your presence fills my days with joy and reminds me daily of the kind of mother I aspire to be. I am profoundly grateful for the positive impact you've had on my life.

To my spirited Sadie Jane, your vibrant and beautiful nature brings so much joy. While you might not have been a big help with my writing, your infectious enthusiasm made every moment special. I am incredibly proud of you and excited for everything you are becoming.

Lastly, to my sweet husband Daniel, thank you for your unwavering support of my dreams. Your encouragement and your steadfast relationship with Jesus Christ have been a cornerstone of my journey. Your leadership and love guide our family in the direction that God intends, and I am so blessed to walk this path with you.

To each of you, I extend my heartfelt gratitude. Your love, support, and presence have shaped this book and my life in countless ways. I love you all more than words can express.

Introduction

The world has always told us that beauty is a type of exceedingly valuable currency. As we look at and read fairy tales and the popular fashion magazines, I really believe the narrative is clear; being attractive or pretty opens doors, creates plenty of opportunities, as well as paving the way to tremendous success. What if that narrative is only a small part of the story? What if that elusive allure of beauty hides a seriously complex web of multiple challenges, misconceptions, and unseen struggles in our future self.

In a society bogged down and obsessed with appearances *It's Not Always Smart to be Pretty* delves into my own personal life of those that seem to have it all. I've discovered that behind the glossy exterior of one's true self we witness reality that is often ignored. Most commonly the pressure to maintain an image, the shallow and sometimes difficult relationships that are built on superficial admiration including the somewhat constant battle against the ultimate fear of losing our most promising attribute "our looks".

It's Not Always Smart to be Pretty challenges us today to rethink and process our most concerning values and to question the inherent emphasis we place on our own true physical appearance. It undoubtedly reveals the true beauty that lies not in how we look at ourselves, but ultimately, it's who we are including that deep down strength we find while embracing our authentic selves. I never knew my true self or the countenance to understand who I was behind a beautiful face. The balance between beauty and unintelligence were so far from each other in my own mind.

As you turn these pages and explore, prepare to see beyond the murky surface and discover the hidden truths in the shadows of beauty. This is an infallible book of self-resilience, self-discovery and the ultimate courage to break free from the constraints we place on each other, including myself. Because in the end; it's not the prettiness, or the intelligence that transcends and defines us, it's the prettiness and intelligence in our own hearts and minds that will truly matter.

Please embrace your true worth and remember to celebrate all aspects of your true self while acknowledging that your own individual values extend beyond your physical appearance. You are your own amazing, complex person worthy of love, respect, and admiration for all that you are in this world.

Skating Through Life on My Looks

Chapter One

Wwe all harbor those fleeting moments of memory that sweep elegantly or sometimes crash suddenly into the quiet corners of our minds from our earliest, most impressionable days. Despite our efforts to make sense of them, they slipped through like whispers of wind through an ancient forest, elusive and full of mystery. My journey began at a very young age, my path toward enlightenment and the sometimes-complex grasp of what my life was to unfold.

If you were to ask my parents, they'd tell you it all began at Women's McGee's Hospital in Pittsburgh, Pennsylvania, on March 28th—the day I was born. Weighing in at 8 pounds 3 ounces and stretching 19 inches long, I quickly became known as a precious and stunningly beautiful little girl with bright blue eyes.

My family and friends would often describe me as having a sweet, caring nature and a quiet personality. As I grew up, it became routine to receive a slew of compliments, each expressed with sincere, if exaggerated, admiration. Whenever I received a compliment, my mother would prompt me, "Janie, what do you say?" With a slow, deliberate eye roll showing my mild annoyance, I would sweetly reply, "Thank you." Even as a child, I questioned the necessity of such exchanges, marveling at how early on I recognized that there was so much more to me than just my pretty face and blue eyes.

During my childhood, I was inseparable from my mom. Whenever my dad would suggest taking us to the park, saying, "You need a break, I'll take the kids to the park," my mom would often choose to stay behind and get some cleaning done. Without hesitation, I'd choose to stay with her, passing up the trip with my siblings and dad. The appeal of spending time with her, even if it meant doing chores, was far stronger than any adventure outside the house. I was a true mama's girl.

While my brothers and sister would eagerly run to get their shoes, I would be there, tightly wrapped around my mother's ankles with an iron grip, unwilling to let go. In my young mind, my presence beside her was never in question—I belonged there. I was convinced that no matter what her plans were, they included me. I followed her from room to room, and whether she was vacuuming the living room or washing dishes in the kitchen, I was her constant shadow.

Wherever she went, I made sure to be right there with her, as though we were two pieces that belonged together. A significant part of our connection, at least in my eyes, had to do with the timing of my mom's life-changing decision to give her heart to Jesus. She was pregnant with me when she made that commitment, and I always felt that, because I was physically connected to her at that moment—quite literally attached to her by the umbilical cord—I had received a little bit of Jesus, too. We shared something significant: the moment of her spiritual rebirth. In some small way, I felt like I was part of that moment, after all, I was right there, growing in her belly, while she accepted Jesus into her heart.

As I grew older, though, I noticed that my mom really did need breaks from time to time. I remember one moment when she gently looked at me and said, "Janie, mommy is in timeout." It was a phrase that carried weight in our household. "Timeout" was not just for kids—it was for her, too. It meant that she needed quiet, uninterrupted time for herself. I did not fully understand the gravity of what it meant for her to need a break, but I respected it. It was the one time when I gave her the space she asked for without question. I might not have liked it, but I knew that when Mom was in timeout, it was serious.

Looking back now, I realize that those moments of "timeout" were crucial for her sanity. Being a mom to four kids while managing the house and balancing the countless responsibilities that came with raising a family, must have been exhausting. But at that age, all I saw was that she was my mom—the person I wanted to be near every second of the day.

Yet, in those quiet moments when she needed space, I learned something invaluable. I learned that even the people we love need room to breathe. It took me a while to grasp that concept, but slowly, I began to understand that giving someone space doesn't diminish the love or connection—it will actually strengthen it. And while those "timeouts" may have been hard for me at the time, they were probably the only times I truly respected her boundaries, even if I didn't fully grasp their importance back then.

As I mentioned before, I have an older sister, an older brother, and a younger brother. My sister was somewhat of an untouchable figure during my formative years, the role model. She was the smart one, brimming with a confidence that always made her seem perfectly composed. My parents were clearly very pleased with her; she never caused any trouble or stress. In my young, impressionable eyes, she had set a high bar.

This image of an untouchable sister was, of course, shaped by my own perceptions. A vivid memory that sticks with me is from when we received our progress reports in elementary school. Watching my sister present her report to our parents, I could see the relief and pride on their faces—a look of satisfaction that seemed to say, "We have a child who will succeed." It often seemed that during parent-teacher conferences, we always attended my sister's first. She would consistently receive accolades and praise for her intelligence.

I have a distinct memory of one parent-teacher conference that I will never forget. My sister, my parents, and I were waiting in the school hallway when my sister's teacher called her name with great enthusiasm and said to my parents, "Watch this." She then recited an incredibly long, complex sentence about Snoopy, the beloved dog from the Charlie Brown cartoon. At first, I couldn't follow where the sentence was going, but the teacher then asked my sister to identify the nouns, pronouns, adjectives, determiners, verbs, adverbs, prepositions, conjunctions, and interjections within it.

Without missing a beat, my sister confidently dissected the sentence, leaving the teacher speechless. To make things even more impressive, the teacher pointed out that one of the words could function as another part of speech. True to form, my sister, ever the debater, launched into a detailed discussion, confidently asserting that the word didn't fit the suggested pattern—backing it up with solid reasoning. Watching this exchange, I became convinced that my sister was destined to be a teacher. My parents, beaming with pride, looked on with visible joy.

Parent-teacher conferences for me always had a different tone. As soon as my parents sat down, the teacher would begin with, "Mr. and Mrs. Torbich, Janie is so beautiful, her eyes are just stunning. She is such a sweet child, never causing any problems in class—so cute and kind." My dad's expression would brighten instantly. His typically quiet demeanor softened, and he'd give a small, contented nod, his eyes wrinkling at the corners with a wide, proud smile. My mom, sitting beside him with her back straight and her legs crossed neatly, would graciously accept the compliment, giving a slight, elegant nod. Her hands rested calmly in her lap, but with a quick tilt of her chin and a steady, focused gaze, she would redirect the conversation. "Yes, she is a beautiful child, and thank you," she would say, her tone measured yet warm, "but that is not why we are here. We would like to know more about her academic performance—how is she doing in class?"

My teacher, in that gentle way teachers sometimes speak when they are particularly fond of a student, explained to my parents, "She is struggling with reading and comprehension. She is worked extremely hard on her sight words, but she is still having difficulty sounding out new words."

I could sense my mom's disappointment, and the long, quiet ride home felt heavy as I tried to process what had just happened at the parent-teacher conference. I overheard her say from the front seat, "Andy, we've got to work with her at home." Then she added, "Maybe it's her eyes." I remember thinking, Mom, how could my pretty eyes make me dumb? She turned to me and asked, "Have you had trouble seeing your books or worksheets at school?" I told her I thought I could see just fine, but soon after, we were at the eye doctor, getting my vision tested.

Looking back, I now understand that my mom was not questioning my intelligence. She was simply searching for answers—trying to figure out why learning seemed harder for me. At the time, though, my young mind could not fully grasp the concern behind her actions.

My mom was already managing a lot—juggling the demands of three children. It was hard for her to give me the focused attention I needed for my schooling. Still, she decided on a plan. Every night, she told my dad that I needed to read to him and my little brother, so I could work on my words and comprehension. This became a special time for me, lying on the floor with my dad and little brother, practicing my reading while we all settled in together. But as much as I loved that time, my dad, exhausted from his long workdays, would often fall asleep midway through my reading. When he drifted off, my motivation would wane, and I found myself putting in less effort, knowing my audience was not fully awake.

I kept reading, slowly working my way through the basic sight words—*the, is, a, and*—all the while glancing at my dad, waiting for him to wake up. Every night, without fail, my mom would check in and find him dozing off on the floor beside me. With a gentle touch, she'd nudge him awake and quietly say, "Janie's skipping words again." He would stir, blinking his eyes as he struggled to shake off sleep, then sit up and try to refocus, guiding me through the words I was missing. Even though they had their hands full with my siblings, they somehow made me feel like I had their undivided attention in those moments. I realized just how much they believed in me.

When my brother was four years old, he could read better than I could, which was remarkable for someone his age. Despite his ability being impressive, I couldn't help but feel left out and inadequate as a reader. He had a favorite book, and I often assumed he had just memorized the words because my dad would guide him, teaching him where to point. Yet somehow, my brother always seemed to know what the words were. I often wondered, is he really reading them or just memorizing them? My dad would proudly take that book everywhere, telling everyone, "My son can read!"

But when it came to me, my dad's focus was never on how smart I was. He rarely ever bragged about my intelligence when we were out. Instead, his attention was on my appearance. He would introduce me by saying, "This is Janie, my beautiful daughter—look at her stunning blue eyes!" It became clear to me that people noticed and commented on my physical attributes more than anything else. In those moments, my little brother, even at such a young age, could sense my disappointment. Although he did not fully understand why, he always showed compassion, offering comfort in his gentle, caring way.

Throughout elementary school, my teachers would continuously pass me on to the next grade, even though I struggled academically. In fourth grade, my mom attended one of those parent-teacher conferences, eager to hear about my progress. I remember sitting quietly, listening as my teacher smiled and said, "Janie is so beautiful, incredibly sweet, and a bit quiet when she is working through things in class. But she is still having difficulty with her academics."

Despite the compliments, my mom's expression tightened. She was not pleased to hear that I was being passed on to the next grade without fully mastering the material. The praise was not enough—she wanted to know that I was truly learning and understanding what was being taught.

I do not recall all the details of that day, but I vividly remember my mom pulling me down the long school hallway, passing classroom after classroom, looking anxious, and upset. I had no idea where we were going, but that day marked the end of my time in elementary school. I never went back. My mom kept me home for a week, and at first, I felt free and thrilled—no more early mornings or school routines! But after a few days, I started to miss my friends.

One day, my mom came home with a surprise: schoolbooks. She was going to teach me at home. I remember asking, "Mom, is this even legal? Can we do this?" Little did I know homeschooling was perfectly legal, and my mom was fully prepared to give it her all. She poured her heart into teaching me, even though I was significantly behind in my studies. Soon, a friend from church started coming over twice a week to help with my reading, which became a much-needed outlet for learning and improvement.

I have fond memories of my younger brother scooting up next to me as I read, eager to learn alongside me. It was during those moments, with my family by my side, that I found joy in learning and began to regain my confidence. Despite the progress, I still felt the weight of my struggles, and I often doubted myself.

Watching my brother learn words that I should have already known left me feeling inadequate. However, my mom never gave up on me. She was my rock, always offering encouragement, even when I felt overwhelmed and defeated.

There were times when the pressure I placed on myself, coupled with my mom's determination, became too much, and I would break down in tears. My mom, juggling so many responsibilities with my siblings, sometimes needed a break from the intense teaching sessions. But she always came back, steadfast in her commitment to help me succeed.

As part of a homeschool group, we had to take standardized tests at church. I remember taking the End of Grade (EOG) test and feeling a sense of accomplishment when I completed it. Up until then, I had always felt confident in my physical abilities. But mental confidence? That was something I had struggled with for years. Despite knowing I had a pretty face, I lacked confidence in my ability to learn.

The following year, I returned to public school, and my reading had improved significantly, thanks to my mom's dedication to homeschooling me. I took a grade placement test, and, to my delight, I was placed in the grade I needed to be in—sixth grade. My parents were incredibly proud, and I could see the sense of accomplishment on their faces, especially my mom's.

In middle school, I worked hard, passing my classes with C's and D's. My mom continued to be my constant support, creating flashcards, making up rap songs to help me memorize information, and being the coolest mom and teacher. Although I was still passing by the skin of my teeth, I skated through school until eighth grade, when things came crashing down.

My eighth-grade English teacher, Mrs. Lassiter, saw right through me. She didn't just see a pretty girl—she saw someone who was struggling beneath the surface. I couldn't stand her; it felt like she was always picking on me. Eventually, she ended up failing me.

Failing the eighth grade was devastating, and I kept it a secret for a long time—it was too embarrassing to admit. Failure is a word I never wanted to associate with myself, and owning up to it was incredibly painful. Deep down, I knew I had not put enough effort into my schoolwork. I was more focused on my appearance and social life than on my studies, and it came back to haunt me.

The hardest part was knowing my friends were moving on to high school while I was left behind.

I ended up spending four years in middle school instead of three. After repeating eighth grade, I finally passed and made it to high school. By then, I had learned to lean on my appearance to get by in school. Teachers liked me, and I assumed that no one could see past my blue eyes to the struggles I faced academically.

In ninth grade, my mom once again took matters into her own hands. Determined to give me the education I deserved, she pulled me out of public school and enrolled me in a private school where I received one-on-one attention. This time, I was ready for a change. I was ready to be smart, to stop relying on my looks to get by. My mom was relentless in her pursuit, sacrificing her own time and energy to ensure I had the support I needed.

My grades improved dramatically in private school. For the first time, I saw an A on my report card, and it was the first time I truly felt capable. I kept pushing forward, and by the time I graduated, I had A's, B's, and only one C.

After high school, I pursued my passion for cosmetology, and I thrived in that environment. I worked hard, excelled in my classes, and even made the Dean's List. My mom continued to be my champion, standing by my side through all my struggles and triumphs. She is, without a doubt, the strongest woman I know.

In my eyes, my mom was the epitome of beauty and grace—her intelligence and business acumen unmatched. I admired her deeply, striving to follow her example in everything I did. As I progressed through cosmetology school, I found myself not only excelling in the academic portions but also thriving in the hands-on aspects. I embraced every challenge with determination, fueled by the desire to live up to the ambitious standards she had always modeled for me.

I was the youngest in my class, but that did not deter me from giving my all. My passion for the craft grew with every passing day, as I honed my skills and worked hard to perfect every technique. There was something thrilling about the process—taking a vision and turning it into reality with just a comb and a pair of scissors in hand.

One day, my mom came to visit me at school, eager to see how I was doing. The excitement I felt was indescribable; I wanted nothing more than to make her proud. As luck would have it, my teacher, Mrs. Faye, took that moment to share her thoughts on my progress. She praised me effusively, calling me not only quick and efficient but also naturally gifted with hair. I remember the way her words washed over me, each compliment sinking in deeper than the last. Mrs. Faye went on to describe me as a sweet and hard-working student, someone she believed was destined for great things.

Hearing those words in front of my mom was like a dream come true. I had always yearned for moments like this, where my hard work was recognized and validated. The overwhelming sense of pride I felt at that moment was beyond anything I had experienced before. It was as if all the effort I had put into my studies and practice had culminated in this single point of affirmation. I felt truly smart, capable, and seen for more than just my potential. It was a day that left an indelible mark on me, inspiring me to push forward with even more passion for the path I had chosen.

Cosmetology had always been my chosen path, a world where skill and creativity converged. From the beginning, I understood that this field would require constant hands-on work, something I was eager to embrace. The realization dawned on me one day as I practiced yet another technique—I can do this. It was not just about becoming proficient with scissors and combs; it was about knowing deep in my heart that I could make a mark, not only in my career but in the world. For the first time, I had the potential to become something significant in my chosen profession.

Those were busy days, juggling school, and work, yet I thrived in the intensity. While I was fully immersed in cosmetology, perfecting my craft, I was also working at a gym—a place I had been part of since I was just 13 years old. My passion for fitness and health had grown alongside my love for beauty. It was not enough to excel in one area; I wanted to conquer both worlds. I was fascinated by the way the human body worked, not just aesthetically, but functionally. This passion led me to pursue a personal training license and a degree in fitness and nutrition.

The gym had become more than just a job; it was a place where I could blend my love for fitness with my drive for success. Every day, I pushed myself to learn more, train harder, and prove my worth in an industry that I felt equally passionate about. My hard work eventually paid off when I was offered the role of Gym Manager. It was a proud moment, a testament to my dedication and the countless hours I had poured into both my education and my job.

However, that moment of achievement was quickly overshadowed by a familiar sting. The gym owner, a woman I had worked with for years, saw my potential—but not in the way I had hoped. Instead of recognizing my business acumen or the work ethic that had earned me the manager position, she fixated on something else entirely. In her eyes, I was not the young professional she had mentored but a beautiful girl with striking blue eyes. She even went as far as suggesting that I should marry her son, not because of my capabilities but because of my looks. It was a frustrating reminder that, once again, my merit was being overshadowed by my appearance.

This was a moment that could have sent me spiraling, questioning my worth. Why couldn't I be seen for my intelligence, my hard work, and my drive? Why was I so often reduced to my looks, even when I had proven myself in my career? It was a disheartening realization, but it also fueled a deeper determination in me to keep pushing forward, to ensure that one day I would be recognized for who I truly was—beyond the surface.

I ended up marrying her son. He was very handsome and into bodybuilding, just like me, and we both loved working out. In fact, he proposed to me at the gym while I was on the elliptical— he had just gotten off work and stopped by to surprise me. Eventually, though, we divorced. He wanted me to stay home and focus on family life, and I do not blame him for that. But I had my own goals, dreams I wanted to pursue, and I felt I could not do that as a mother at the time. The divorce was incredibly difficult, and a lot of rumors spread that were not true. Looking back, I realize I could have managed things differently.

Later, I found out that his mom thought very highly of me— she knew I was smart and appreciated for my work ethic and for me helping grow the gym. I love her and miss her dearly. She gave me an incredible opportunity when I was just 13, and for that, I will always be grateful.

I was working at the gym when I met a woman named Danielle. She was new to the area, and her kind nature was immediately apparent. One day, I was helping in the gym's daycare, and she expressed some concern about leaving her little boy in the care of someone she did not know well. I reassured her, promising to keep a close eye on him. Unfortunately, just a brief time later, her son had a mishap—he accidentally hit himself in the lip with a Thomas the Train railroad track, leaving a noticeable scar. I remember feeling terrible, rushing into the gym to get Danielle, thinking she would be upset or disappointed. But to my surprise, she was incredibly understanding, brushing off the incident with a kindness that I hadn't expected.

That was the beginning of our friendship. Danielle became a constant presence in my life, someone who saw me differently than others did. She wasn't fixated on my appearance but instead recognized the intelligence and drive that I had long buried. She saw potential in me beyond what was on the surface, and that realization was like a breath of fresh air. Her encouragement gave me the confidence to revisit my ambitions, and she often praised my ideas and plans for the gym. We started working out together regularly, and in those moments, she helped me rediscover the passion I once had for learning and achieving goals. Danielle's wisdom and insight pushed me forward in ways that no one else had before.

As our friendship deepened, I found that my confidence was no longer tethered solely to my looks. Working at the gym became a place where I could blend both aspects of who I was—my appearance and my intellect. People sought out my advice not only for fitness and nutrition but also for tips on their hair. It was a strange but fulfilling balance, and for the first time in a long while, I felt like I was both beautiful and smart—capable of anything.

Then, just as I was hitting my stride, the gym—the place that had become a home to me—began to change. I watched as the ownership shifted hands multiple times. Each transition brought a new set of challenges, as the gym that I had grown to love slowly morphed into something unfamiliar. It was a bittersweet time, knowing that the place where I had regained my confidence was no longer the stable ground it once had been. But even through the changes, I held onto the lessons I had learned and the friendships I had forged, knowing that no matter where life took me next, I had finally found my footing again.

At that point in my life, I found myself during unexpected transitions and challenges. The gym, which had been my second home for so long, had changed hands after the tragic loss of the previous owner. His death shook everyone, and though one of my coworkers took over as the new owner, the atmosphere was never quite the same. Despite this, I continued working hard, managing the gym, and selling memberships with the same drive that had fueled me for years. Then, without warning, the gym closed, and for the first time, I felt a sense of powerlessness. This moment was a turning point for me—a realization that I could no longer rely on just getting by. I needed to take control of my path and stand firm in who I was.

Before the gym closed, my life was a whirlwind of commitments. I was balancing the salon, working at the gym, and a position in a nearby company's customer service department. My main responsibility was handling account receivables, but I also took on some sales and advertising tasks. My mom, ever the supportive figure, played a significant role in helping me land the job. She prepared my resume and submitted it to the owner, who was an old family friend, my sister used to babysit for his kids. I had a strong feeling that it was my mom's connections, rather than my qualifications, which secured the interview and the job.

On my first day, I walked into the office with nervous anticipation, only to be greeted by the awkward stares of seven men seated at their desks. It was immediately clear that I had entered a male-dominated environment, and it made me feel out of place. I eventually met Jack, the Manager, who showed me to my desk, which was located on a platform that overlooked the men in the parts department. The office had a strange setup, with my desk positioned as if I were on display. In the beginning, I tried to keep my head down and focus on the job, but it was not long before the stares and comments became impossible to ignore.

The first few weeks passed without incident, and I even got along well with the woman I worked closely with. However, as time went on, I noticed a shift. Her attitude toward me changed drastically, and I could feel her growing resentment. At first, I couldn't figure out why, but eventually, the pieces fell into place. The attention I received from the men in the office had started to cause tension. It became increasingly obvious that their visits to our desk area were more about seeing me than addressing work-related concerns, and it wasn't long before my coworker began blaming me for the disruptions.

One day, I was called into Jack's office, where I found my coworker already seated. She wasted no time airing her grievances, claiming that the male employees' behavior had become a distraction and that it was my fault. She argued that the men were neglecting their work, forgetting to clock in and out, and even causing her more work because of their constant interactions with me. She also blamed me for the increased customer traffic, insisting that people were only coming by to purchase items so they could have an excuse to visit our desk.

As I sat there, listening to her accusations, I felt a wave of disbelief. It wasn't my fault that these men were behaving unprofessionally, and yet, I was being blamed for their actions simply because of how I looked. When Jack turned to me for my thoughts, I tried to explain the situation, pointing out that I had done nothing to encourage this behavior. I even confronted my coworker, asking why she believed it was my responsibility to manage how others acted. Her response left me stunned—she said that my appearance was the problem, as if I had any control over that.

After the unresolved meeting and ongoing frustrations at work, I confided in my mom about how I felt devalued and insulted. I told her how disheartening it was to be judged for my appearance rather than my abilities, and how much I wanted to prove that I had more to offer. Thankfully, my mom had once worked a similar job and had an incredible knack for teaching me the ins and outs of the role. She became my lifeline during that time, always available to guide me through any confusion or questions I had. With her help, I mastered the tasks and responsibilities that had once felt overwhelming, and before long, I was performing better than my coworker, who had become so cold toward me.

My mom wasn't just a source of support at work—she also became my protector from the unwanted attention that seemed to follow me. She would frequently laugh and tell me how guys at the office would approach her, asking about me. She had no problem turning them down, always with the same firm reply, "Believe me, she needs no help." Her strength in these situations was empowering, and I knew she had my back through it all.

But the attention wasn't just a minor inconvenience—it became emotionally draining and, at times, terrifying. I remember feeling trapped by the constant advances, as if my friendliness was being misconstrued as something more. There were moments when I found myself cornered by someone professing feelings I didn't reciprocate. It felt like no matter how hard I tried to remain professional and focused on my work, the line between my job and their desires kept blurring in their minds. I wasn't interested in them, yet they seemed to expect something from me, all because of how I looked.

One day, things escalated beyond what I could have imagined. A coworker, who I had politely turned down before, became aggressive after my rejection. He cornered me at the end of the workday, refusing to let me leave or even clock out. His voice grew louder and angrier as he hurled accusations at me, demanding to know why I wouldn't go out with him. Fear washed over me as I stood there, helpless and scared, waiting for my mom to arrive. When she didn't see me come out after waiting for over ten minutes, she walked into the warehouse and saw what was happening.

In that moment, my mom became my hero. She raised her voice, cutting through his rage with a power that instantly silenced him. "My daughter is not some piece in your monopoly game," she said, her words striking like lightning. "You will not pass go, and you will not collect $200." I will never forget the way she commanded the room, telling him in no uncertain terms that his behavior was unacceptable. She turned to me with a calm, firm voice and said, "Let's go, Janie," and then turned back to him, declaring, "Game over."

That day, something shifted within me. I saw firsthand the strength of words, the power they could wield when used with conviction and purpose. My mom had taught me more than how to navigate a difficult job—she had shown me how to stand up for myself, how to use my voice to reclaim my power. I realized then that this wasn't the environment I wanted to be in. It wasn't healthy, and I deserved better. No job was worth staying in if it meant working alongside people who disrespected me and tried to control me.

The experience became a pivotal lesson, one that stayed with me long after I walked away from that toxic workplace. It was about more than escaping a bad situation—it was about learning to define my worth on my terms, not anyone else's.

You Are Not My Brightest, But You Are My Prettiest

Chapter Two

If you were to ask my dad when he first started to worry that I was not going to make it in life, I know he would never admit it. He is too kind-hearted for that. But I can tell you the exact moment when that seed of concern was planted in his mind. It was back in middle school, in the seventh grade, after a Friday night football game.

As a typical teenager, I was more focused on my social life than anything else. My dad had picked me up after the game, and I remember saying quick goodbyes to my friends before hopping into the car. He asked me, as he often did, "How was the game?" I barely looked at him when I replied with a curt, "Fine."

We drove in silence for a while, the car filled with that awkward teenage energy that parents know all too well. Then, out of the corner of my eye, I noticed a man on the side of the road burning something in a barrel. The smell of burning trash soon filled the car, carried by the wind. I wrinkled my nose in disgust and turned to my dad.

"That man is so rude," I huffed. "He could at least turn the barrel around."

My dad gave me a sidelong glance, then turned his eyes back to the road. He did not say anything at first, trying to figure out if I was serious. After what felt like an eternity, but was only a few minutes, he finally broke the silence. "Are you kidding me right now?" I met his gaze, completely serious. "Nobody wants to smell that. He could easily be more respectful and just turn the barrel the other way."

My dad glanced at me, and I could see the realization dawn on his face. He was trying to decide whether to laugh or to worry. Finally, in the calmest voice he could muster, he explained, "Janie, the smoke from the barrel is going to go whichever direction the wind is blowing. The man cannot control that."

I sat there, stunned into silence, my teenage arrogance deflated by his simple logic. I did not say another word for the rest of the drive home. My dad did not push the conversation further, but I imagine that moment stuck with him. It was the first time he saw how sheltered and naive I could be. It was then that he began to worry just a little about how I would navigate the real world, where not everything—or everyone—would bend to my will.

Looking back, I can almost laugh at how ridiculous I must have sounded. But I also wonder if that was one of those moments that shaped my dad's quiet concerns, the ones he never voiced but carried with him all the same.

As I got a little bit older, I became a little bit more serious about different circumstances and how I would handle them. That event calmed me down somewhat to help me understand I didn't have control of everything! I remember it like it was yesterday. This event most definitely taught me a good lesson in life and in remembrance gave myself confidence in how to navigate my job hunting; not to expect to control those insights, but to help me reimagine them in a positive light. One night I was scrolling through job listings, looking for something new and exciting, when I stumbled across a description that caught my eye: "Customer Service Representative Needed for a Finance Company." Immediately, I thought, this is it. I want to be a finance girl. Without hesitation, I decided to make the call. It was the first job I reached out to that day.

The day was a cold one in January, colder than most in North Carolina. It had snowed the night before, which was a rare sight for us. But our snow was not the soft, powdery kind; it was more like ice, making the roads slick and treacherous. Despite the hazardous conditions, I felt compelled to seize this opportunity. I could feel my nerves tingling with excitement and anticipation as I dialed the number listed on the ad.

When I called, only one person answered. It was the manager, the only person who had braved the icy conditions to make it into the office that day. There was a certain energy in his voice, a curiosity, as he asked me if I could come in for an interview right away. He mentioned how he loved my enthusiasm and the spark in my voice—something I was known for, especially when I was excited about something.

I did not even hesitate. I bundled up, threw on my coat, and braved the icy roads. The drive was slow, each turn requiring careful navigation over patches of ice, but I could not help feeling a surge of adrenaline. This was my chance, and I was not going to let a little snow or ice get in my way. The streets were empty, a testament to how bad the weather was. I passed a few cars that had slid off to the side, but I pressed on, determined to make it.

When I finally arrived at the office, I parked and made my way to the front door, my breath visible in the chilly air. The parking lot was almost deserted, which made me second-guess whether I had the right place. But as I walked up, I noticed the lights on inside, just one solitary figure moving about. I knocked on the door, which was locked, and after a moment, the manager came to let me in.

He opened the door and looked at me, seeming a bit surprised but also impressed that I had made it there despite the weather. Before I could even introduce myself or say hello, he blurted out, "Are those contacts?"

I was momentarily taken aback by his question, but I quickly gathered myself. With a smile, I replied, "No, sir, these are my real eyes."

He looked at me for a moment longer, and then he smiled— a warm, genuine smile that seemed to light up the room. That unexpected question broke the ice, quite literally, and set the tone for the rest of the interview. It turned out to be one of the best interviews I had ever had. I walked out of there feeling confident and excited about the possibility of joining the finance world.

From that moment, I knew I was on the right path, even if it meant navigating through ice and snow to get there.

I was used to receiving compliments. Everywhere I went, people noticed something about me—my eyes, my smile, my energy. But that day, as I stepped into the building, I was not there for compliments; I wanted to be recognized for my intelligence and potential. I wanted to prove that I was more than just a pretty face.

After several compliments from the manager about my appearance and my bubbly personality, we finally got down to business. We talked in detail about the role and what my responsibilities would be, as well as the possibilities for growth within the company. He was eager to know more about what I could bring to the table and how I could contribute to the team. He seemed impressed by my answers and enthusiasm, nodding as I spoke about my willingness to learn and grow.

As we wrapped up our conversation, he leaned back in his chair, a thoughtful expression on his face. "I really like you," he said, as if he was still processing the words. "I think you would be a great fit here. I have been interviewing candidates for a few months now and have not been able to find the right person. But I have a great feeling about you. I felt it from the moment we spoke on the phone." His sincerity was evident, and I could feel my heart swelling with hope.

He went on to explain that although he wanted to move forward, I would need to have a second interview with the CEO of the company, Jim. He reassured me, saying he was confident about my chances and that he would speak with Jim to set it up as soon as possible. "I believe my search is finally over," he said with a smile. "You're the one I've been looking for."

The next day, which happened to be a Thursday, my phone rang. It was the manager, sounding just as upbeat as he had the day before. "We'd like to bring you in for a second interview," he said. "This time, you'll be meeting with Jim, the CEO."

I could sense a mixture of excitement and nerves bubbling up inside me as I prepared for the interview. I wanted to make a strong impression on Jim, to show him that I was not just enthusiastic but also capable and driven.

When I arrived at the office, I was introduced to Jim, a distinguished and professional businessperson who exuded confidence and authority. He greeted me with a firm handshake and led me into the office. We made some small talk to break the ice, and then he got straight to the point.

"Where do you see yourself in ten years?" he asked, his eyes focused intently on me.

I paused for a moment, considering my answer. I wanted to be bold and confident, to show that I was ambitious and not afraid to aim high. With a slight smile, I replied, "The CEO."

Jim raised an eyebrow, clearly taken aback by my response. For a moment, I was not sure if I had gone too far, but then his serious expression softened into a smile. I could tell he appreciated my confidence and determination. We continued the interview, discussing my background, my skills, and what I hoped to achieve in the role. He asked tough questions, but I felt prepared and answered them with honesty and enthusiasm.

By the time I left the office, I felt a mix of exhilaration and uncertainty. Had I made the right impression? Did I say enough to convince Jim that I was the right fit for the company?

The following Monday, my phone rang. It was the manager, and I could hear the excitement in his voice. "Congratulations!" he said. "Jim was very impressed with you, and we'd like to move forward with the hiring process. We just need you to complete a drug test and fill out some paperwork."

I felt a surge of joy and relief wash over me. I had done it! I had proven myself. I quickly scheduled the drug test appointment and filled out all the necessary paperwork. The home office conducted a background check, and everything came back clear.

On February 15th, 2010, I officially started my new job. It was the beginning of a new chapter, one where I could prove that I was more than just a friendly voice or a pretty face. I was determined to show them—and myself—that I had what it took to succeed in the finance world.

I started my journey as the Customer Service Representative (CSR) of the company, and I could not have been prouder. It was not just a job for me; it was a chance to prove myself, to step into a role that required more than just a friendly smile or a pleasant demeanor. It was an opportunity to display my skills and my work ethic.

Jim was a pivotal figure in my early days at the company. He never made me feel like my appearance was the most important thing about me, and for that, I was grateful. Unlike others, Jim did not shower me with compliments about my looks. He was different. He saw me for who I was beyond the surface, and I respected him immensely for that. Whenever people around the office would comment on my eyes or make remarks about my appearance, Jim would playfully steer the conversation away from my looks.

I remember one day vividly. I was at the front desk, handling calls and paperwork, when a man walked in to make a payment. As he approached, his eyes widened in surprise, and he exclaimed, "Wow, look at those eyes!" He was clearly taken aback by my appearance. I prepared myself for the usual string of compliments, but Jim, who was nearby, quickly stepped in with his usual wit.

Without missing a beat, Jim looked up and said, "What's wrong with her eyes?" His tone was light, almost teasing, but there was an underlying message that I understood perfectly. Jim was not dismissing me or the man's compliment; he was reminding everyone that there was more to me than just my looks.

I could not help but smile at Jim's remark. It was not just a deflection—it was his way of ensuring that I was valued for more than just my appearance. He understood that being constantly complimented on how I looked could sometimes overshadow my professional capabilities. By redirecting the focus, he allowed me to stand out for my work and my dedication rather than just my appearance.

There were many moments like this in the office. Whenever someone would mention my eyes or my smile, Jim would gently shift the conversation. He would joke around, asking, "How many compliments have you gotten today?" It became a running joke between us, but beneath the humor, I could sense Jim's genuine effort to ensure that I felt seen and appreciated for my talents and hard work.

He created an environment where I could thrive based on my skills and contributions to the team. He knew how to strike the perfect balance—acknowledging the compliments while making sure I knew that my real value lay in what I brought to the company. His subtle yet consistent efforts made me feel respected and empowered, something that had a profound impact on my confidence and how I viewed myself in a professional setting.

Working under Jim's leadership, I learned to embrace my role with confidence, knowing that I was more than just a face behind the desk. I was a vital part of the company, contributing to its success in meaningful ways. His support helped me grow, not just as a professional, but as a person who understood her worth went far beyond her appearance.

Later, I had the chance to meet the man who owned the company, Council, Jim's father. He was an impressive figure, someone who immediately commanded respect not just because of his position but because of the story behind it. Council had started the finance company at the age of 55—a time when most people are thinking about retirement, not launching a new venture. He had spent most of his career working for others, learning the ropes, gaining experience, and biding his time. Then, one day, he made a bold decision: he decided it was time to step out on his own and build something from the ground up. His determination and willingness to take such a significant risk so late in his career were inspiring. It was clear that he was a man of vision and ambition, someone who knew what he wanted and went after it with unwavering focus.

Council was not only successful; he was also incredibly kind and generous with his knowledge. He had a sharp mind and a reputation for being extremely strict when it came to work. He demanded excellence, but he was also fair. You could tell that he valued hard work and dedication more than anything else, and he had little patience for anything less than one's best effort.

One day, I made a silly mistake at work. I cannot even remember what it was now—something minor, but it caught Council's attention. He got my attention, and I braced myself for what I assumed would be a stern reprimand. Instead, he looked at me with a half-smile and said, "You're not my brightest, but you're my prettiest."

The comment caught me off guard. I did not know how to react. Part of me wanted to laugh it off, to take it as a compliment. But another part of me felt a sting. His words stayed with me long after he left. I had mixed emotions about what he said. On one hand, it felt nice to be acknowledged, even in a lighthearted way. It was a compliment. But on the other hand, it bothered me. It diminished my intelligence, to place my value on something as superficial as looks.

I remember thinking to myself, at least I am something. But as the day went on, his words kept echoing in my mind, and they began to bother me increasingly. Why do I have to be one or the other? Why do people so often see beautiful and not smart, or smart and not beautiful? Why can't I be both?

The more I pondered this, the more I realized that I did not want to be pigeonholed. I did not want to be defined by just one characteristic or quality. I wanted to be seen as a whole person— someone who was both attractive and intelligent, both personable and competent. I did not want to be forced into a box or reduced to a stereotype.

Council's comment, whether he intended it or not, was a wake-up call for me. It made me reflect on how people perceived me and how I wanted to be perceived. I was determined to show everyone that I could be both pretty and smart, that these qualities were not mutually exclusive. I wanted to break down those stereotypes and prove that a woman could be multi-dimensional.

From that moment on, I approached my work with renewed determination. I made a conscious effort to demonstrate my capabilities and intellect. I sought out more opportunities to gain experience, to challenge myself, and to show that I was more than just a face behind a desk. I wanted to earn respect for my skills and my ideas, not just for how I looked.

I started taking on more responsibilities, volunteering for projects that required critical thinking and problem-solving. I asked more questions, engaged more deeply in meetings, and made sure that my voice was heard. I wanted to make an impression, to show that I had the brains to match my beauty.

Over time, I did notice a slight shift. My colleagues began to see me in a different light. They started coming to me for advice, valuing my opinions and insights. Council, too, seemed to take notice. His comments became more about my contributions and less about my looks. It was a subtle shift, but it meant the world to me.

In the end, I realized that being pretty and being smart were not mutually exclusive. I could be both, and I could excel in both. I learned that I did not need to choose one identity over the other. I could embrace all aspects of who I was and let my true self shine through, confident in my abilities and proud of who I had become.

The owner of my company, Council, passed away on February 1st, 2015. His death was a profound loss for everyone who knew him. For me, it felt like the end of an era, and I could not help but worry that I would never get the chance to truly prove myself to him. Council had seen something in me—a potential that I was only just beginning to understand and harness. With his passing, I feared that the opportunity to demonstrate my full worth was gone, that I would never get to show him how much I had grown or how capable I was beyond just being "the prettiest."

After Council's untimely death, his sons took over the company, John and Jim. I noticed right away that Jim was different from his father in many ways, but in others, he was strikingly similar. Unlike his father, he never commented on my looks. He never said, "Your eyes are beautiful," or "You look nice today," or even complimented me on my upbeat personality. Instead, he took a different approach—one that was challenging yet refreshing. From the moment he took over, he was direct and straightforward. He would hand me a file and say, "Look at this deal and tell me what you would do." Or he would pull up a credit report and ask, "Would you approve this or not?" Every day brought a new challenge. He would say, "How would you manage this situation? What would you do with this customer?"

At first, I was taken aback. His father had always been kind and gentle in his guidance. Council's son, on the other hand, was all about business, about getting things done and done right. But I soon realized that he was doing something incredibly valuable: he was teaching me how to think critically and solve problems

45

independently. He did not just want me to agree with him or follow his lead; he wanted me to develop my own voice and opinions. He encouraged me to think for myself and to not shy away from complex decisions.

It quickly became clear that he valued my intellect, my critical thinking skills, and my capacity to learn. He saw potential in me that I did not even fully see in myself at the time. He saw a smart, young woman with drive, determination, and an insatiable desire to learn more and to be more. He saw that I was not content with just staying in one place—I always wanted to push forward, to improve, and to take on more responsibility.

He would challenge me regularly, not in a condescending way but in a way that made me realize he was pushing me to grow. I would present a solution to a problem, and he would ask, "Did you consider this?" His constant questioning and challenging used to frustrate me to no end. I would think I had everything figured out, only for him to offer a distinct perspective or point out something I had not thought about. It was like he was playing devil's advocate, not because he wanted to undermine me, but because he wanted to teach me how to think strategically and independently.

I remember so many times telling him, "This is what I think we should do," only for him to respond, "Have you considered all the angles? What about this scenario?" It was maddening at times, but it taught me to never take anything at face value, to always dig deeper, and to consider every possibility. It became clear that he was training me to manage things on my own, to be confident in my decisions, and to not rely on anyone else to solve problems for me. He was teaching me how to be a leader.

I knew then that I was not destined to sit at the front desk as a customer service representative my entire life. I was not going to be content with just answering phones and taking payments. I had more to offer, and he saw that in me. I began taking on more responsibilities, proving repeatedly that I wanted to climb higher, to do more, to make a real impact on the company. He continued to trust me increasingly, letting the line out a little bit at a time, evaluating my limits and giving me room to grow.

With each small mistake I made, it felt like the end of the world to me. I remember confessing my errors to him, bracing myself for a reprimand, but he never pulled back his support. Instead, he used every mistake as a learning opportunity, asking me what I had learned and how I would manage things differently in the future. It was as if he knew that these mistakes were a necessary part of my growth, that without them, I would not learn and evolve. I felt safe under his guidance. He was like my mother, who always pushed me to be better, like Mrs. Lassiter, who had failed me in eighth grade because she knew I had more to give, and like Mrs. Huff (whom you will meet later in this book), who saw the potential in me when others did not. He found out how I understood things and tailored his teaching methods to suit my learning style.

One day, he used an analogy that stuck with me. He took his hands, held them up, and touched his fingertips together, saying, "This is your brain." Then he crossed his fingers over each other and touched the fingertips of his crossed fingers together, adding, "And this is other people's brains." At first, I did not understand what he meant. His brain was straight, mine was straight, but others were twisted. It seemed like a strange way to explain things. But after thinking about it for a while, I asked him to clarify.

He simply said, "Look it up." So, I did. I learned that a "twisted brain" could mean someone who is mentally or emotionally unsound or disturbed, while a "straight brain" referred to someone who is straightforward, direct, holding to a proper course or method. As time passed, I found myself often saying, "What's right is right, and what's wrong is wrong." To me, this simple phrase became more than just a statement about ethics; it became a guiding principle. It represented a straight-minded approach to life—knowing right from wrong and making decisions based on that understanding.

He saw in me a woman who could distinguish between right and wrong, who could stay on a straight path even when things got complicated. He understood the importance of simplicity and clarity, and he encouraged me to embrace these qualities in my own thinking and decision-making processes. In many ways, he was unlike any boss I had ever met. He was caring and generous, but he also believed in his employees and wanted them to succeed. He was the kind of leader who would rather go without than see his team struggle.

I remember once, a coworker who was an assistant manager at one of the offices needed her roof repaired. Without hesitation, he bought her a new roof, knowing how important it was for her family to have a safe and secure home. His generosity and understanding went beyond material things; he knew the importance of family and personal responsibilities.

When my dad had to have surgery, my two brothers went up to Pennsylvania to be with him, but I stayed back to take care of my niece. He understood how important this was to me, and he allowed me to pick her up every day at 3 p.m. on my lunch break. She would come back to the office with me, do her homework at my desk, and stay until my workday was over.

He did not have to make these accommodations, but he did because he cared about his employees as people, not just workers. He knew that supporting his team in their personal lives would lead to a stronger, more resolute workforce. And he was right. I felt a loyalty to him and to the company that I had not felt before. I wanted to succeed, not just for myself, but for him, for the trust he had placed in me, and for the opportunities he had given me.

Under his guidance, I grew not only as an employee but as a person. I learned the value of challenging work, of critical thinking, and of always striving to be better. I learned that being a leader was not just about giving orders but about setting an example, supporting others, and challenging them to be the best versions of themselves. He showed me that there was more to me than I had ever realized, and for that, I will always be grateful.

Beyond the Surface: Redefining Beauty

Chapter Three

Beauty is such a subjective concept, often defined differently by each person. Who are we to say what beauty is? What I have come to realize is that beauty is not just about appearances or the surface-level qualities that society often values. It is much deeper than that, encompassing actions, intentions, and the authenticity with which we live our lives.

Growing up in my household, my mother had a clear and straightforward approach when it came to how we presented ourselves. She was never one to sugarcoat her opinions, especially when she believed that we were not putting our best foot forward. It was not unusual to hear her say things like, "Go change your outfit; those colors don't match," or "That's way too much makeup; you need to take it off." At first, her bluntness often felt jarring, as if she were being overly critical or harsh, especially when all we wanted was a bit of freedom to explore and express our personal style. In those moments, it was easy to feel misunderstood or even stifled, as if our attempts at self-expression were being dismissed without consideration.

However, as I grew older and gained more perspective, I began to see the deeper wisdom behind her words. My mother's comments were not intended to diminish our self-expression or creativity; instead, they were rooted in a genuine desire to guide us toward a more thoughtful understanding of how we presented ourselves to the world. She passionately believed that the way we chose to dress and carry ourselves was more than just a matter of fashion or appearance. To her, it was a true reflection of our inner selves—our values, self-respect, and the care we took in how we wanted to be perceived by others.

Over time, I came to appreciate the lessons she was imparting. Her words were not meant to tear us down but to build us up with a stronger foundation of self-awareness. She taught me that constructive criticism, even when it stings, can be a powerful tool for growth. Her approach helped me realize that true beauty transcends the superficial aspects of physical appearance. It is not just about the image you see in the mirror or the clothes you choose to wear. Instead, it is about the way you carry yourself—the confidence you exude, the respect you command, and the authenticity you project in every interaction.

My mother's teachings instilled in me a deeper understanding of the connection between our outward appearance and our inner selves. I learned that the choices we make in how we present ourselves are a reflection of our character and values. The confidence and authenticity we project are not merely products of our physical appearance, but of the self-assurance that comes from knowing who we are and what we stand for. In this way, my mother's influence helped shape not only my sense of style but also my sense of self, reminding me that true beauty is found in the harmony between the two.

Her approach instilled in me the importance of being mindful about my choices—not just in fashion, but in all aspects of life. I learned that presenting myself in a way that aligns with who I am on the inside is a powerful form of self-expression. It is about choosing clothes that make you feel comfortable and confident, and wearing makeup that enhances rather than masks who you are. Her advice taught me to embrace my individuality and to present myself in a way that is true to my character, values, and beliefs. In reflecting on her guidance, I realize that my mother's words were a lesson in understanding the deeper essence of beauty. They encouraged me to look beyond the surface, to appreciate the value of self-reflection and self-awareness, and to strive to present myself in a way that is a genuine expression of who I am. This wisdom has stayed with me throughout my life, reminding me that true beauty is not about perfection or adherence to societal standards but about authenticity, integrity, and the way we carry ourselves through the world.

My mom's advice did not stop at appearances. I often call her for guidance, especially when it comes to handling personnel at work—a task that can be one of the most complicated parts of running a business. Yet, somehow, she always manages to turn the conversation back to me, asking, "What were your actions? How did you manage it? Did you explain it clearly so they could understand what you wanted them to do?" Her approach is not about placing blame but about fostering self-reflection and growth. And you might wonder why I continue to seek her advice. It is because she never lets me down; her insights always lead to a beautiful outcome. By making me look at myself and my own actions, she reminds me that, in the end, I am the only one I can control.

Through the lessons imparted by my mother, I have come to understand that beauty encompasses much more than just physical appearance or societal standards of attractiveness. It is not merely about conforming to trends or meeting external expectations. Instead, true beauty involves a deeper, more personal journey.

Beauty, as my mother taught me, is fundamentally about being honest with oneself. It starts with an introspective look at who you are, acknowledging your own likes and dislikes, and understanding what genuinely resonates with you. This self-awareness is crucial because it allows you to align your external presentation with your internal values and preferences. It is not just about looking good; it is about feeling authentic and comfortable in your own skin.

Moreover, beauty is about having the courage to make changes when necessary. It means being open to evolving and adapting as you learn more about yourself. This might involve adjusting your style, shifting your perspectives, or even confronting aspects of yourself that need growth. Embracing change can be challenging, but it is a vital part of the journey towards a more genuine expression of beauty.

Beyond personal appearance, beauty also extends to how we interact with the world around us. It is reflected in our behavior, our kindness, and the respect we show to ourselves and others. How we treat people, the empathy we extend, and the integrity with which we live our lives contribute significantly to our overall sense of beauty. It is about creating positive connections and leaving an impression through our actions and attitudes.

Beauty is a harmonious blend of self-awareness, authenticity, and meaningful interactions. It is a multifaceted quality that emerges when we align our inner values with our outer presentation, and when we engage with the world in a way that reflects our true selves. This broader perspective on beauty has helped me appreciate that it is not a static attribute but a dynamic and evolving part of who we are.

When I think about what truly defines beauty, I remember the saying, "Beauty is in the eye of the beholder." This phrase suggests that beauty does not exist independently; "the observer creates it." What is pleasing to one person's eyes might be seen as ordinary or unattractive to another. Therefore, beauty is not defined by what people think or say; it is defined by what you think of yourself. You are the beholder, and your perception is the only one that truly matters.

When I was a child, I had a Barbie doll, which was a gift from my grandma. Considering my grandma had a lot of grandchildren—my father being one of twelve—you can imagine how chaotic Christmases were. My parents let me keep the Barbie, even though I am not sure it was entirely age-appropriate at the time.

Barbie, with her perfect hair and fashionable clothes, was beautiful, but she represented something more than just a pretty face. Barbie was a symbol of ambition, showing me that I could be anything I wanted to be. She had over two hundred careers, from astronaut to entrepreneur, breaking through barriers in a way that inspired young girls like me. In 1973, Barbie became a surgeon when very few women were entering operating rooms. By 1985, she was a CEO, symbolizing women breaking through the glass ceiling. Barbie's forays into STEM fields were designed to inspire girls to explore science, technology, engineering, and mathematics. So yes, she was pretty, but she was also incredibly smart and versatile.

However, Barbie has always been a subject of controversy, particularly regarding her body and appearance. This criticism arises because women often compare themselves to idealized images, even a doll, from an early age. Instead of finding beauty in who we are, we start looking to others and creating a skewed image of what beauty should be. Comparing ourselves is a losing battle. We are always looking for things we lack and, eventually, end up comparing ourselves to others based on incomplete or inaccurate information.

Let me give you a visual example: I was on the beach with my mom about twenty years ago. We had just finished running and were cooling down before heading back to her condominium for some floor exercises. The beach was almost empty that day, but suddenly, a woman walked by with her toddler. She was a beautiful lady, very fit and well-put-together, wearing a classy cover-up and a big, sassy hat. I started to go on and on about what I saw: "Mom, that lady probably has a huge house and a perfect little family." I created an entire scenario in my head: her husband was at their older son's football game, and they were killing time before heading home to make lunch for the family. I had absolutely no information about her but constructed an entire narrative based on her appearance.

When we got back to the condominium, my mom told me she knew the woman. She then shared the real story: the woman did not have any children of her own. In fact, she had suffered two miscarriages, and the small child she was with was her sister's, whom she babysat every Saturday to make a little extra cash. Her husband had left her six months ago because she became so depressed after her miscarriages. She lost her job after consistently showing up late. Now, she was living with her sister and brother-in-law because she had no other place to go. I did not believe my mom at first and asked how she knew all of this. She said, "Janie, she was my co-worker." That moment was eye-opening for me. It made me realize how wrong I was and taught me that beauty is never as it seems.

This experience taught me a valuable lesson about perception and the assumptions we make based on outward appearances. It reminded me that true beauty is found in understanding, compassion, and empathy—not in how someone looks or the story we create about them in our minds.

We define beauty with our actions every day. It is about more than just an image or a stereotype. True beauty is when people are genuinely kind, when they take action to help others, and when they live authentically, not confined by societal standards. It is about knowing your worth, standing by your values, and not letting others define you. Beauty is in the actions we take, the way we treat others, and how we choose to live our lives. It is ever evolving, growing deeper and more profound as we do.

I have an aunt who truly embodies beauty, not just in her appearance but in her heart and actions. What defines beauty for me is kindness, and Aunt Donna has always shown that in abundance. She never forgets a birthday, Easter, or Christmas, going beyond to make each occasion special. Growing up, I often thought she was a superhero—I could not understand how she managed to do everything she did with such grace.

When my parents went through their divorce, my mom and I took a trip to Pennsylvania. Despite the emotional challenges, my mom was always so kind and thoughtful, asking if there was anyone on my dad's side I wanted to see while we were there. Without hesitation, I thought of Aunt Donna. Even now, as an adult, I think of her often and realize how much she has influenced my life in positive ways.

We did not always write letters or say thank you as often as we should have, and sometimes we did not seem as appreciative as we truly felt. But Aunt Donna's kindness was unwavering, and she continued to be a source of love and support. My parents trusted her completely, allowing us to have cousin sleepovers at her house when we were young. Those times were filled with laughter, comfort, and a sense of security that I still cherish today.

Even though I do not see her as much now, especially since I have become an adult, my admiration for her has only grown. Aunt Donna taught me that true beauty lies in kindness, consistency, and the love you give to others. I am so grateful for the example she has set and for all the ways she has touched my life.

As I reflect on all these experiences and the lessons I have learned, I realize that beauty is indeed a powerful concept. It keeps us wondering and is also blinding. When someone notices you, they often create an image in their head based on superficial observations. But true beauty is much deeper than that—it is about authenticity, kindness, and the courage to be you. It is about looking beyond the surface and seeing the world and people around you for who they truly are.

In my journey, I have discovered that true beauty is not something to be chased or compared; it is something far deeper, more personal, and unique to each of us. It is not about conforming to society's standards or trying to fit into a mold that someone else has created. Instead, beauty is about embracing who we are, in all our imperfections and uniqueness. It is about living authentically and expressing our true selves through our actions, our kindness, and our integrity.

Beauty shines brightest when we are kind to others, when we lift each other up rather than tear each other down, and when we choose to act with grace and compassion. It is in the little moments—like offering a helping hand, listening without judgment, or showing empathy and understanding—that our inner beauty is truly revealed.

We all have the power to define what beauty means to us. It is not confined to physical appearance or external validation but is found in the strength of our character, the depth of our love, and the courage we show in being ourselves. When we embrace this idea, we allow ourselves to be seen as we truly are, flaws and all, and in doing so, we empower others to do the same.

By living this way, we help create a world that values acceptance over judgment, compassion over criticism, and authenticity over perfection. In this way, we contribute to a world that is not only more accepting but also more beautiful, where everyone feels valued and seen for who they truly are. This is the beauty that transcends time and trends—the beauty of a life lived with purpose, love, and genuine connection to others.

When I reflect on the people who have had a profound impact on my life, one name stands out prominently: Don Fregeau, better known as Diesel Don from Good Works Auto Sales. Don was much more than a mentor; he was a devoted friend, confidant, and someone whose words carried a weight I do not think he fully realized. I can still hear his voice, full of encouragement and wisdom, always reminding me of my worth and potential. His favorite line, which he often repeated to me, was that I was the "cream of the crop." For a long time, I did not fully grasp the depth of this phrase. However, after his passing, its meaning became clearer and more profound than I could have ever imagined.

The phrase "cream of the crop" refers to the best or most excellent individuals or things within a particular group. It originates from the idea that cream rises to the top of milk, symbolizing that the best qualities or individuals stand out from the rest. When someone says, "the cream of the crop," they mean that the people or items being referred to are the best of the best, distinguished by their superior quality, skill, or performance.

Don came into my life during a time when I was still discovering myself, particularly in terms of my intelligence. I had always struggled with the feeling that I was not smart enough, constantly measuring myself against others. I would look in the mirror and see someone who could rely on their looks, but deep down, I craved something more—something that went beyond outward beauty. It was Don who saw the potential in me and was direct enough to challenge me to confront those feelings head-on.

I vividly remember one Saturday while deeply engrossed in authoring my book, I wrestled with how much of myself I wanted to reveal. I had written many words, but something about them felt surface-level, as if I were holding back. It was easier to gloss over my deeper insecurities and present polished versions of my struggles. Then, unexpectedly, Don called me. We talked for three hours, and this call was different from the usual ones. His voice carried an urgency and sincerity that immediately grabbed my attention.

"I've been thinking about you," he said. "And the Holy Spirit told me to call you. You are not going deep enough into your story; you need to go deeper. Do not be afraid to discuss how you felt. I know it will mention a lot of hurt, but it is time to finally give it to God and let go. This book is you laying it down at His feet."

His words stopped me in my tracks. It was as if he had tapped into the very struggle I was facing—how much to reveal and how raw to be in my storytelling. Don, with his usual clarity and directness, was not just encouraging me to keep going; he was urging me to dig deeper, to be more vulnerable, and to confront the parts of my story that scared me the most. He believed in the power of my story and knew that if I could express it fully, it would resonate not just with me, but with anyone who read it.

"You've got something important to say," he continued. "And your story is meaningful. Don't hold back."

That phone call changed everything for me. It was like a switch flipped in my mind, and I realized that if I didn't go deeper, if I didn't confront my own insecurities about intelligence and worth, I would be doing a disservice not only to myself but to the people who needed to hear my story. Don was right—my story had significance.

Don had this remarkable ability to see beyond the surface and into the heart of things. He knew how to encourage yourself in a way that did not just make you feel good but also made you think, reflect, and push yourself further. He was not content with half-efforts, and he did not want that for me either. He pushed me because he believed in me, in my story, and in the impact it could have.

I cannot even count the number of times he would tell me, "The cream always rises to the top." He would say it with a knowing smile, as if he could already see my future and knew that I would find my place, even when I doubted it myself. For the longest time, I thought it was just a metaphor he used to make me feel better. I understood that cream rises to the surface, but I did not fully grasp what he was trying to convey until much later.

What Don was really saying was that no matter the obstacles or self-doubt, the true value within me—the intelligence, the worth, the potential—would always find a way to rise above. The best qualities, the ones we sometimes do not even realize we possess, cannot be hidden for long. They will emerge, just like cream rises to the top of milk, no matter how much it is stirred or shaken. Talent, virtue, excellence—all those things that make us who we are—will eventually be recognized, even if it takes time.

Don's belief in this principle was not just something he said to me; it was something he lived. He had built his life and career on that same foundation, following in the footsteps of his father, who had also sold cars. Don was not just any car salesperson; he was exceptional because he genuinely cared about people. He had a way of making everyone feel valued, whether they were buying a car from him or simply talking to him. And that is what he did for me—he made me feel like I mattered.

What made my bond with Don even more special was our shared family dynamic. Don was one of four children, just like me—two boys and two girls in each of our families. This commonality created an unspoken connection between us, a mutual understanding that comes from growing up in a similar family structure. Although we rarely spoke about it, this shared experience added an extra layer of understanding and closeness between us.

Don was also an incredible musician, with albums and bands to his name. Whenever we did deals together, customers would come into my office and rave about how Diesel Don's music had touched them. Don once told me he wanted me to see my book through, just as he had wished to see his music through.

I miss Don more than words can express. His passing, due to complications from COVID-19, hit me hard. At 72, he had lived a life rich with wisdom, generosity, and a deep love for those around him. Losing him felt like losing a piece of myself, but I find comfort in knowing his legacy endures, not just in my life but in the lives of countless others he touched.

One of the greatest blessings is watching his daughter, Spring, continue his legacy. She has taken over Good Works Auto Sales, ensuring the business remains vibrant and true to its roots, just as her father would have wanted. I am incredibly proud of her and deeply grateful. Whenever I visit the lot, I find myself in the office where Don and I had so many meaningful conversations. It feels as though he is still there, guiding us both and reminding us of the life lessons he imparted about faith, perseverance, and living fully.

I am so thankful for Spring and her husband, David. They understand how much Don meant to me, and Spring and I have become remarkably close. It feels as though she is a living connection to Don, and I cherish our friendship deeply. We relate to each other in so many ways, and I know that both Spring and David would support me in achieving anything I set out to do. Continuing to do business with Good Works Auto Sales is especially meaningful to me; each deal feels like a tribute to Don's memory and keeps his spirit alive in our hearts.

Don's influence is woven throughout the pages of my book. Every time I wanted to give up or questioned whether my story was worth telling, I could hear his voice reminding me, "Your story means something." And it does. Because of Don, I found the courage to be honest about my struggles with intelligence and self-worth. His impact is a lasting testament to his belief in me and his dedication to encouraging others to rise above their doubts.

Realizing the Brain Behind the Beauty

Chapter Four

In a charming village surrounded by rolling hills, lived a young woman named Beauty. Beauty was celebrated for her remarkable good looks, but she often felt overshadowed by the expectations that came with it. She yearned for recognition beyond her appearance and dreamed of a life where her mind and heart could be appreciated.

One day, Beauty's father, a humble merchant, found himself in trouble when he wandered into a mysterious and foreboding castle deep in the forest. The castle was owned by a reclusive figure known as the Beast, a creature with a fearsome appearance and a dark reputation. The Beast demanded that one of the merchant's family members take his place as punishment for the intrusion. Beauty, determined to protect her father, bravely volunteered to go in his stead.

Upon her arrival at the castle, Beauty was met with an intimidating figure— the Beast. Despite his gruff exterior, the castle was filled with wonders that intrigued Beauty: grand libraries, intricate inventions, and rare artifacts. As Beauty explored the castle, she discovered that the Beast was not only knowledgeable but also enthusiastic about learning. He had spent years studying various subjects, from literature and science to philosophy and art.

Beauty and the Beast began to spend time together, engaging in deep conversations about their interests. Beauty was initially taken aback by the Beast's intellectual prowess. He spoke eloquently about his studies and shared his ideas with genuine enthusiasm. As their conversations continued, Beauty realized that the Beast's fearsome appearance was a mere facade for a brilliant and compassionate mind.

The more Beauty got to know the Beast, the more she admired his intelligence and creativity. She found herself captivated by his insights and began to value their conversations above anything else. In turn, the Beast appreciated Beauty's curiosity and intellect. Her genuine interest in his work made him feel valued and understood for who he truly was.

As Beauty and the Beast grew closer, Beauty began to see beyond her own superficiality. She realized that she had often been seen only for her beauty, rather than for her intelligence or character. The Beast's wisdom and their mutual respect helped Beauty understand her own worth and potential, beyond her physical appearance.

One evening, as they sat together in the castle's grand library, the Beast shared his own story. He had once been cursed not only for his outward appearance but also for his vanity and disregard for others. The curse could only be broken by finding someone who truly valued him for his inner qualities, rather than his outward form.

Moved by the Beast's story and their shared experiences, Beauty, and the Beast both recognized that true beauty lies in understanding and appreciating each other's inner selves. Their bond deepened into a profound connection based on mutual respect and genuine affection.

In time, the curse was lifted, and the Beast transformed into a handsome prince. However, both Beauty and the prince knew that their bond had been forged not through appearance but through their shared intellectual and emotional growth.

In the end, the story of Beauty and the Beast beautifully illustrates that true beauty and value lie not in outward appearances, but in the depth of character and the strength of emotional and intellectual connections. Their journey teaches us that genuine love and understanding can reveal the true essence of individuals, leading to profound personal growth and transformation. By looking beyond superficial traits and embracing the inner qualities that define us, we find that real worth and happiness come from recognizing and valuing the beauty within ourselves and others.

As I got older, I learned that real beauty does not start on the outside. It begins within, in the mind. Beauty, in my view, is more about how we see ourselves from the inside out. Does that make sense? Beauty starts in the brain, with how we think and what we believe. "What your brain thinks, your eyes will believe." In other words, what we think is what we will end up believing.

Let me explain it like this: Imagine waking up in the middle of the night, disoriented and wiping sleep from your eyes. It is dark, and you are unsure whether it is day or night. You feel incredibly thirsty and head to the kitchen. As you open the fridge for a drink, out of the corner of your eye, you think you see a Man standing there. Your heart races, fear kicks in, and for a moment, you believe there is someone there. But then, in a split second, you realize it is just a winter coat you threw on the rack earlier, with a hat on top.

In that brief moment, your eyes saw something, and your brain almost made you believe it was real. This is how our minds work. What we think is what we believe, and that can shape how we see the world—and ourselves.

The challenges we face in life can feel like a bird soaring through the sky, sometimes touching down briefly, not sure if it is at the start or end of its journey, and unsure of itself. It is hard when you do not fully know or accept who you are. That uncertainty can make the road ahead tough to navigate. But when you understand and embrace who you are, it helps your inner beauty shine. Real confidence comes from knowing that God created you with a purpose. Psalm 139:14 says, "I praise you because I am fearfully and wonderfully made; your works are wonderful, I know that full well."

I have learned that I am more than just a pretty face. When I saw the substantial numbers on our sales reports and realized that every goal, we set at work was achieved, I understood that those results were proof of my hard work. You do not always have to be front and center for people to recognize the effort you are putting in. The reward is knowing that your achievements are being noticed, even if you are not always in the spotlight.

As I kept pushing forward, working hard, and staying focused, people began to see more than just my looks. They saw that I am also intelligent, capable, and serious about what I do. It was a moment of clarity for me—I realized that I had so much more to offer the world. My beauty was not just about how I looked, but also about the smart, diligent person I had become.

Compliments about my looks were common, and while they were flattering, they also shaped my identity in a way that I did not fully understand until much later. I began to believe that my value was tied to my appearance. People saw the beauty on the outside, but I constantly questioned if there was anything more to me beyond that.

From an early age, I was aware of the power that beauty held. It opened doors, drew attention, and provided opportunities. Yet, beneath the surface, I harbored a persistent insecurity: the fear that I was not smart enough. Despite the outward confidence my looks seemed to give me, I struggled internally with feelings of inadequacy when it came to my intellect.

In school, I often felt unseen. My peers who achieved top grades and won academic awards were celebrated for their intelligence. They were the ones whose names were called during award ceremonies, whose essays were read aloud in class as examples of excellence. They were chosen for advanced programs and special projects, and their accomplishments were highlighted in newsletters. Teachers spoke of them with a certain pride and admiration that seemed reserved exclusively for academic achievers.

Meanwhile, I felt overlooked, like my strengths and talents were not as valuable because they did not fit neatly into those categories. It seemed like the students who excelled in academics had a brighter light shining on them, while others, like me, were left in the shadows. No one celebrated creativity, emotional intelligence, or the ability to connect with others on a deeper level. The focus was always on grades and academic success.

This left me wondering if I had anything to offer. I worked hard, but my achievements did not look like theirs. I did not realize at the time that intelligence comes in many forms—emotional, creative, and even practical intelligence are just as valuable as book smarts. It took me years to understand that my strengths were not in the test scores or academic accolades, but in the way I could think creatively, connect with others, and bring a different kind of value to the table. Now, I know that those things are just as important, even if they were not always recognized in school.

It seemed that while others were praised for their intellectual achievements, my worth was tied solely to how I looked. No one asked me about my thoughts, my dreams, or my aspirations. No one seemed interested in the ideas I had or the questions I wanted to explore. My identity was reduced to a surface-level characteristic, and I struggled with the feeling that I was being seen but not truly seen.

I remember watching my classmates receive praise with a mix of admiration and envy. I admired their dedication and intelligence, and I envied the recognition they received. They were seen as the future doctors, engineers, Finance company owners, writers, and leaders. They had a clear path paved with their academic successes. In contrast, my path seemed less defined, less certain. I often wondered if my looks would be enough to carry me through life, and the thought filled me with a deep sense of unease.

I questioned whether I could ever measure up to my peers who were celebrated for their brains. There were moments in class when I knew the answer to a question but hesitated to raise my hand, fearing that my response would be dismissed or that my classmates would think, "What does she know? This self-doubt became a self-fulfilling prophecy, holding me back from fully engaging in my education and from believing in my own potential.

During my state board exam for cosmetology, I passed— and for the first time, I did not cheat, rely on my looks, or need my mom to write a note for me. This experience sparked a new passion for learning within me. I started challenging myself, reading more, and actively seeking opportunities to expand my knowledge. I realized that intelligence, much like beauty, is not something fixed or given, but rather something that can be developed and nurtured over time. This was the beginning of my journey to utterly understanding my own potential.

As I pursued my education and career, I encountered many people who continued to comment on my appearance. But now, their compliments did not hold the same power over me. I had discovered a deeper, more fulfilling source of self-worth. I knew that my value was not limited to my looks, but was enriched by my intelligence, my curiosity, and my willingness to learn and grow. I also began to focus on my studies with renewed determination. I sought out subjects that intrigued me, pushing myself to excel not for external validation but for my own growth and fulfillment. Each small step built my confidence and slowly shifted the perception of those around me.

This journey was not easy. It took time for me to break free from the idea that I had to fit into a certain mold. I had to push past the fear of being judged and embrace the discomfort of challenging myself. There were moments of doubt, but each step forward brought me closer to discovering my true potential.

Looking back, I realize that the journey of discovering my intelligence was just as crucial as learning to embrace my beauty. These aspects of who I am are not at odds with each other; they exist in harmony, each enriching the other in ways I never fully understood until now. I used to see them as separate entities, competing for recognition and validation, but I have come to see that they are interwoven threads in the rich tapestry of my identity.

As I reflect on my past, I remember watching my classmates receive praise with a mix of admiration and envy. It was not just about the accolades they received—it was the way they seemed to embody qualities I longed to fully understand and appreciate within myself. In those moments, I struggled with the idea that I needed to choose between being seen as intelligent or beautiful, not realizing that my worth was not limited to one or the other.

Today, I am proud of who I have become—not because of how others perceive me, but because of the deep understanding and acceptance I have cultivated about myself. The realization that beauty and intelligence are not mutually exclusive has been liberating. It has allowed me to embrace all facets of who I am with confidence and joy.

To anyone who feels confined by the narrow expectations of beauty or intelligence, I offer this message: You are so much more than the surface-level judgments or stereotypes that others might impose upon you. Your mind is a powerful, beautiful force, brimming with potential for growth and achievement. Do not let yourself be boxed in by others' limited perspectives. Embrace your unique talents, nurture your intellect, and let yourself shine in all the ways you were designed to. Remember, you are wonderfully made, both inside and out, and it is in embracing every part of yourself that you truly come to realize your full potential. Let this be your call to step boldly into the fullness of who you are, celebrating every aspect of your being and shining brightly in the world.

The True Meaning of Being Smart

Chapter Five

Smart: is a word we encounter constantly, woven into the fabric of our everyday lives. We hear it in the halls of schools, where children are praised for being smart if they ace a test or solve a tricky math problem. We hear it at work, where colleagues are commended for their smart decisions or innovative solutions. It pops up in casual conversations when someone shares a clever insight or a quick-witted remark. The media is also filled with stories about geniuses who have changed the world or achieved extraordinary success. But what does it really mean to be smart? Is it simply about having a high IQ, scoring well on standardized tests, or excelling in academic pursuits? Is it the ability to think quickly on your feet and offer a sharp response in a conversation?

The reality is that the concept of being smart is far more nuanced and multifaceted than these traditional measures suggest. Being smart is not just about memorizing facts, mastering textbooks, or solving complex equations with ease. It encompasses a wide range of qualities, including emotional intelligence, creativity, critical thinking, adaptability, and the ability to learn from experiences. Intelligence can manifest in various forms—sometimes as practical wisdom, sometimes as deep empathy, or even as the capacity to innovate in unexpected ways. In truth, being smart is less about what we know and more about how we apply that knowledge in diverse situations, how we interact with the world around us, and how we use our unique skills to contribute meaningfully to society.

When I was still in school, I thought I had a clear understanding of what it meant to be smart. In my young mind, being smart was synonymous with academic perfection—achieving straight A's, scoring 100% on every test, and flawlessly completing every assignment. A truly smart person never needed help, and I saw needing assistance as a sign of weakness. This belief drove me to push myself relentlessly, always striving for that unattainable goal of perfection.

However, this pursuit of academic excellence was not as straightforward as it seemed. The path to being "smart" was filled with challenges and moments of profound doubt. I often found myself lost in a sea of words, struggling to grasp their meanings. The more I tried to understand, the more elusive the concepts seemed to become. It felt like comprehension was just within my grasp, only to slip away at the last moment, like trying to catch a feather in a gust of wind. Each time this happened, my confidence took another hit, and I felt increasingly inadequate.

Adding to my frustration was the fact that my teachers often misunderstood my struggles. When I could not focus or seemed to be daydreaming in class, they assumed I was not paying attention or that I was not interested in the material. They did not realize that my apparent daydreaming was a symptom of my internal battle with comprehension and the anxiety that came with it. I was not disengaged; I was overwhelmed. I was grappling with my own fears of inadequacy and the pressure I had placed on myself to live up to my narrow definition of what it meant to be smart. This misunderstanding only deepened my sense of isolation and inadequacy, making me feel like I was always on the verge of failure, no matter how hard I tried.

Over time, however, my understanding of what it means to be "smart" underwent a significant transformation. No longer confined to the rigid definitions of academic achievement and intellectual prowess, my concept of intelligence began to expand and mature. In today's world, being smart is often linked to the broader idea of success—success that goes beyond just professional achievements or personal accolades. It is about navigating life's complexities with a blend of knowledge, intuition, and emotional intelligence. Being smart means adapting to new challenges, constantly learning, and applying that knowledge in ways that are both practical and innovative.

In our careers and personal lives, being smart involves a dynamic form of problem-solving. It is not just about finding solutions independently but also about recognizing when to seek the input and collaboration of others. True intelligence often requires us to dive deep into our own minds and hearts, uncovering our unique motivations, strengths, and desires. It involves releasing the drive to work with others, allowing us to transcend the narrow confines and constraints that society often imposes on us.

In this interconnected world, being smart also means understanding the value of relationships and human connections. The most groundbreaking ideas and solutions often emerge from meaningful collaboration, where diverse perspectives come together to spark innovation and creativity. These current ideas, born from the constructive interaction of working with others, are essential to achieving our most cherished goals. They help us push past the limitations of what we thought possible, enabling us to grow not just as individuals but as a collective. Being smart today means embracing a comprehensive approach to intelligence—one that values emotional depth, people skills, adaptability, and a willingness to grow alongside others.

But what if true intelligence was about embracing simplicity? Are we trying to redefine what it means to be smart? For a long time, I was tempted to attribute my achievements to being exceptionally "smart." It seemed easier to credit my success to a label that implied I possessed some innate brilliance. Yet, when I take a step back and reflect honestly, I realize that my achievements are not the result of sheer intellectual prowess alone. Instead, they stem from something much deeper and more profound.

My success and joy are fundamentally rooted in the love and support I received from those around me. I am fortunate to have been surrounded by people who saw my potential, believed in me, and encouraged my growth. Their unwavering support provided me with the confidence and strength I needed to navigate the complexities of life. It was this unconditional encouragement that enabled me to develop resilience and become a capable leader.

Being smart, it turns out, is not just about having clever ideas or solving complex problems. It is also about recognizing and nurturing the simple yet profound impact of having a supportive network. The love and encouragement from others gave me the foundation to build upon, transforming me from someone who might have simply drifted through life into a leader who could confidently tackle its challenges. In this way, true success is less about intellectual achievement and more about the depth of connection and the power of being genuinely valued.

Throughout my journey, I have been profoundly inspired by the so many individuals who recognized my aspirations and actively supported my growth. Their belief in me was a catalyst that fueled my own development, and I noticed a transformation within myself. Over the years, my confidence and charisma flourished, evolving from a seed of potential into a vibrant and compelling presence. This transformation was deeply intertwined with the respect and admiration I received from others, often for reasons that initially eluded my understanding.

It became increasingly evident that the driving force behind my hard work was not just my own ambition but the love, trust, and faith that others had in me. As I transitioned into adulthood, I realized that this unwavering support was instrumental in shaping my path. Each compliment and encouragement served as a steppingstone, reinforcing my belief in my own capabilities, and pushing me to strive for greater achievements.

One of the most crucial elements in my personal growth was my ability to recover quickly from setbacks. This resilience was not solely a result of my own inner strength but was significantly bolstered by the emotional support provided by my family and friends. Their empathy, understanding, and encouragement functioned as a safety net during challenging moments, allowing me to recover swiftly and continue moving forward with renewed vigor.

The journey toward becoming the person I am today was deeply influenced by the collective support of those around me. Their faith in my potential provided a foundation upon which I could build, and their support enabled me to navigate the difficulties of life with a sense of confidence and perseverance. It is clear now that the strength I drew from these relationships was a key factor in my ability to grow and succeed.

Reflecting on my journey, I can see the many struggles and limitations I faced in my quest to understand my own intelligence and navigate the boundaries of my perceived world. The process of trying to define what it truly means to be "smart" was fraught with challenges. I fell short of my aspirations, struggling to align my self-perception with the concept of intelligence I had in mind. But what exactly does it mean to be "smart"? How do we establish boundaries around intelligence, and are these limitations merely constructs of our own making?

For a significant period, I felt trapped by what I call the "box of limitations." This metaphorical box was filled with labels such as "limitations," "restricted," and "constrained," which confined me and prevented me from exploring my full potential. It was as though I was ensnared in a small space that dictated what I could and could not achieve. Determined not to remain within these self-imposed confines, I sought ways to break free and redefine my understanding of intelligence.

In time, I came to realize that true intelligence is not about excelling in one area while neglecting others. Instead, it is about achieving balance and integrating several types of intelligence. It is about cultivating a well-rounded set of skills and abilities, rather than focusing solely on one dimension of intellectual prowess. Being smart involves recognizing and leveraging your strengths while also addressing and improving upon your weaknesses. It is about being adaptable and resilient, equipped to manage the complexities and uncertainties that life presents.

Intelligence is not a fixed concept but a dynamic quality that evolves with our experiences and growth. It requires an integrated approach that embraces a spectrum of skills and knowledge, allowing us to navigate challenges with a nuanced and versatile mindset. In embracing this broader definition of intelligence, we can move beyond the constraints of our metaphorical boxes and unlock our true potential.

To anyone who feels constrained by traditional definitions of intelligence, it is important to recognize that intelligence is not limited to a single dimension. Rather, it is a rich tapestry of abilities and attributes that together enable us to make meaningful contributions to the world. Our unique forms of intelligence encompass a wide range of skills, talents, and passions that go beyond conventional measures of smartness. Embrace your distinctive strengths, nurture your passions, and let your curiosity lead the way. In doing so, you will come to understand that being smart is not merely about accumulating knowledge but about how you think, feel, and interact with the world around you.

Intelligence is a multifaceted construct that spans various domains, including emotional, creative, practical, and social intelligence, among others. Recognizing and appreciating these diverse forms of intelligence allows us to celebrate the unique contributions each person can make. By fostering an environment that values and supports a broad spectrum of talents, we empower individuals to pursue their passions and create a more inclusive and innovative society. Embracing the complexity of human intelligence means acknowledging that every unique form of intelligence contributes to our collective growth and understanding.

It is also crucial to understand that intelligence extends well beyond traditional IQ scores or academic achievements. While conventional measures often focus on cognitive abilities like reasoning and problem-solving, the concept of multiple intelligences broadens our perspective to include a wider array of human capabilities. Emotional intelligence, for instance, involves understanding and managing our own emotions as well as empathizing with others. Creative intelligence reflects our ability to think freely and innovate. Practical intelligence helps us navigate everyday challenges with skill and insight. Wisdom encompasses a deeper understanding of life and its complexities.

By redefining what it means to be "smart," we open ourselves to a world brimming with possibilities. We move beyond outdated notions and embrace a more comprehensive view of intelligence. It is not about conforming to a narrow definition but about expanding our perspective to recognize all the diverse ways in which people contribute to the world. Intelligence, in its fullest sense, is about curiosity, adaptability, empathy, and the courage to learn and grow continuously.

As we drive deeper into the exploration and expansion of our understanding of intelligence, it is crucial to recognize that being smart extends far beyond merely assessing what we know or what we can achieve. True intelligence encompasses much more than just accumulated knowledge or specific skills; it involves our capacity to learn, adapt, and forge meaningful connections with others.

To understand intelligence, we must consider how it reflects our ability to make thoughtful choices, nurture relationships, and create a positive impact on the world around us. It is not just about the information we possess but how we use that information to navigate challenges, embrace change, and support those around us. Intelligence involves emotional resilience, creativity, empathy, and the drive to contribute constructively to our communities.

Let us, therefore, broaden our definition of what it means to be smart. Instead of narrowly focusing on traditional metrics or achievements, let us embrace a more holistic view that celebrates all the ways in which we can grow, evolve, and have influence. Each of us brings a unique form of intelligence to the table, and this diversity of thought and ability enriches our collective experience. By acknowledging and valuing these varied expressions of intelligence, we can foster an environment where everyone's strengths are recognized and appreciated.

Growing up as the third child in my family, I was the cherished baby for a while. I basked in the love and attention from my parents and older siblings, feeling like the center of everyone's world. I was a bit spoiled, constantly doted upon and made to feel special. My siblings were like my personal fan club, showering me with affection. I loved being the youngest and all the benefits that came with it.

But everything changed with the arrival of my little brother. Suddenly, all the attention I had grown accustomed to was directed toward this tiny new human. I felt a confusing mix of jealousy and resentment. Who was this new person taking my place? It took me some time to adjust. When my brother was about three years old, I had a conversation with him that changed everything. I told him I wanted to be the baby of the family again. To my surprise, my sweet little brother, with all the innocence of a child, told me I could still be the baby if I wanted to. His simple, kind words filled me with joy and made me see him in a new light. From that moment, our relationship transformed. He was not just my little brother; he became my friend.

Janie Torbich

One remarkable thing about my brother was his ability to read at an incredibly early age. By just four years old, he could read better than I could at that age. I remember feeling a mix of pride and embarrassment, thinking, "How is he so good at this already?" My father would always find books for him to read whenever we were out, and people were always impressed. I sometimes wondered if he was truly reading or just memorizing the words, but either way, it was impressive. I wished my father had encouraged me academically in the same way, helping me with my reading challenges. Instead, he often introduced me as his "beautiful daughter," complimenting my looks rather than my abilities.

Despite my early struggles with feeling unintelligent, my brother and I developed a special bond. I loved buying him clothes and making sure he was the coolest kid in school. I enjoyed spending time with him, even as we grew older, and our lives became more complicated. I often went to parties with him, not as a partygoer but as his ultimate designated driver, ensuring his safety. He appreciated that.

What I thought was a typical teenage phase of drinking escalated into something more serious—drug addiction. The day my little brother went to rehab was the day I felt utterly lost. I was confused and could not understand why he could not just stop. I learned he was being taken to a place called Brunswick Recovery Center in Ash, North Carolina, a facility surrounded by cornfields. Now called Christian recovery in Shallotte North Carolina. While he was there, I found a school project he had done in college, which said that his heroes were our dad and me. Reading that essay, all the anger I had felt towards him melted away. It was a moment of clarity and healing for me, as if God had guided me to find that essay to help me through my struggles. In the essay, he wrote that I was smart and successful, words that struck a deep chord with me.

My brother's story is one of redemption and resilience. He struggled with addiction for many years, a battle that often seemed insignificant. Watching him go through this was one of the hardest things I have ever experienced. I saw the toll it took on him and on all of us who loved him. It was a dark period, filled with worry, tears, and a desperate hope that he would find his way back. Despite everything, I never stopped believing in him. I knew that beneath the struggle was the kind, thoughtful brother who had always been there for me.

This was not just any recovery center—it was a place grounded in faith, offering not only physical and mental healing but also spiritual renewal. At CRCI, my brother found a supportive community that understood his struggles and embraced him with open arms. The center's approach was holistic, combining therapy and, most importantly, spiritual guidance rooted in the teachings of Jesus Christ.

The staff at the center, many of whom were in recovery themselves, were living testaments to the power of faith and perseverance. They created an environment of empathy and understanding, showing my brother that he was not alone in his journey. Through daily prayers, Bible studies, and counseling sessions, he was reminded of God's love and the hope that faith can bring, even in the darkest of times. The center's philosophy was that recovery is not just about breaking free from addiction; it is about rebuilding one's life through a relationship with God, finding purpose, and understanding one is worth as a child of God.

The sense of community at the Christian Recovery Center was unfavorable. Every person there was committed not just to their own recovery but to supporting others on their journey as well. My brother often spoke of how the people he met at the center became like a second family to him. They shared stories, struggles, and victories, all bound together by their faith in God and their commitment to recovery. The power of prayer, fellowship, and mutual support created a transformative environment, allowing my brother to rediscover himself and his purpose.

It was at the Christian Recovery Center that my brother truly found healing. He reconnected with God in a profound way, realizing that his struggles did not define him but rather refined him. With each day, he grew stronger, not just physically but spiritually. He learned to lean on his faith, drawing strength from scripture and prayer, and slowly began to rebuild his life. The staff at the center helped him uncover the roots of his addiction, addressing not just the symptoms but the deeper wounds that needed healing.

After completing the program, my brother did not just walk away with his sobriety; he walked away with a renewed sense of purpose. He felt a calling to help others who were facing the same battles he had overcome. He began volunteering at the center, sharing his story, and offering support to new arrivals. It was not long before his dedication and passion for the work led him to a leadership role. Today, he is the CEO of the very recovery center where he found healing, a testament to his transformation and commitment to helping others find the path to recovery.

What began as a rivalry over who would be the baby of the family has blossomed into a profound friendship and connection that I deeply cherish. My brother has taught me about kindness, selflessness, and the importance of family. His journey from addiction to recovery, from despair to hope, has been an incredible testament to the power of faith and the possibility of redemption. He reminds me every day that with God's help, anything is possible and that no matter how lost we may feel, there is always a way back to the light.

Growing up in a large family with multiple siblings was a unique experience, filled with its own set of challenges and joys. Each of us had our own distinct relationships and dynamics, but we always had each other's backs, no matter what. Among all my siblings, my older brother and I shared a particularly close bond. We were more than siblings; we were best friends, partners in crime, and each other's confidants. He was my protector, the one who always looked out for me. Unlike my younger brother, he knew the truth about my struggles in school—my poor grades and difficulty reading. He would often say, "You're just like me; we're just not good at school." Those words, simple as they were, offered me a kind of comfort. It was his way of showing me that he understood that we were in it together.

My older brother was a natural leader, ambitious and fiercely independent. Whenever he got into trouble, I was always right there beside him, ready to stand by his side. We were like a team, bound by loyalty and love. We spent countless hours playing Indiana Jones, with him always as Indy and me as Shorty. Our backyard adventures felt like epic quests—climbing trees, swinging on vines, and exploring the woods like we were searching for hidden treasure. My brother had a knack for inventing clubs and setting up challenges, and I was always eager to prove myself to him, to show him that I was capable and brave.

When my older brother decided to move to Pennsylvania, I was heartbroken. My best friend, my adventure partner, was leaving, and I could not understand why he had to go. But when he called to tell me he was going to have a baby, my sadness turned to joy. I was over the moon with excitement, knowing that this baby would be so loved by all of us, especially by me. When his daughter was born, I went to visit, and the moment I held her, I fell in love. Looking at her reminds me every day of how special my brother is to me and how much he means to our family.

Both of my brothers, in their unique ways, helped me see beyond my limitations and encouraged me to strive for my best self. My older brother was my steadfast supporter, always there to comfort me when I felt inadequate or struggled with feelings of not being smart enough. He understood my challenges and never judged me for them; instead, he reassured me that intelligence comes in many forms and that school grades were not the only measure of worth. My younger brother, on the other hand, always saw me as smart in his own way. He had this unwavering belief in my abilities, no matter what. His confidence in me was a constant reminder that I was more than my struggles.

Growing up with my brothers taught me that intelligence is not a one-size-fits-all concept. It is not about being perfect in every area or excelling academically to the exclusion of other talents. True intelligence is about balancing and integrating several types of skills and abilities. It is about recognizing that everyone has their strengths and weaknesses and that these do not define our value. Intelligence is about adaptability, resilience, and the ability to navigate the complexities of life with grace and determination.

We often think of intelligence in narrow terms, like book smarts or academic achievement, but it is so much more than that. Intelligence is a rich tapestry of abilities that make us uniquely capable of contributing to the world in meaningful ways. It is about emotional intelligence, social intelligence, creativity, and practical skills that allow us to solve problems and connect with others. By recognizing and appreciating the many forms of intelligence, we can celebrate diversity, empower individuals to pursue their passions, and create a more inclusive and innovative society.

So, embrace your unique intelligence, whatever form it takes. Cultivate your passions, be curious, and let your interests guide you. Remember that being smart is not just about what you know but about how you think, feel, and engage with the world around you. Intelligence is about understanding that every experience, whether it involves climbing trees with your brother or struggling with school, contributes to who you are. Each moment is a lesson, a chance to grow, and an opportunity to show yourself and the world the unique blend of intelligence that only you possess.

This integration sets a profound and reflective tone from the outset, emphasizing the multifaceted nature of intelligence, which is then beautifully illustrated through your personal stories and experiences with your brothers. It creates a cohesive narrative that ties the broader concept of intelligence to your unique family dynamics and personal growth.

So, embrace your unique intelligence, whatever form it takes. Cultivate your passions, be curious, and let your interests guide you. Remember that being smart is not just about what you know but about how you think, feel, and engage with the world around you. Intelligence is about understanding that every experience, whether it involves climbing trees with your brother or struggling with school, contributes to who you are. Each moment is a lesson, a chance to grow, and an opportunity to show yourself and the world the unique blend of intelligence that only you possess.

Redefining My Reflection

Chapter 6

The stories we sometimes tell ourselves often come from the way we feel, and those feelings can shape our entire perception of reality. My younger brother is a fitting example of this. He told me about a time in middle school when he attended a school dance. In his memory, the gym was massive, the size of four football fields, and there were a thousand people milling around. Of course, in reality, his whole school only had about three hundred students. But in his story, that is how it felt—overwhelming.

He spotted a girl he wanted to dance with and, after working up the courage, he crossed what seemed like a never-ending gym floor to ask her. When he finally got there, she turned him down. As he walked back across the gym, he was convinced that everyone was watching, laughing at him. The people by the punch bowl were making fun of him, the girls walking off to the bathroom were whispering and giggling about his rejection, and even the parents chaperoning were pitying him, thinking, "Poor guy."

Years later, when we were both older, he shared this story with me. He explained how he had felt so humiliated that day. But as he recounted it, I realized that none of what he thought was happening had been going on. The guys at the punch bowl were not laughing at him—they were sneaking alcohol into their cups. The girls were walking off, not to make fun of him, but to avoid getting caught up in the trouble brewing at the punch bowl. Even the parents were not pitying him; they were watching the boys at the punch bowl, wondering what they were up to.

When he finished telling me the story, I laughed with him and said, "You didn't really feel that way, did you?" But he looked at me seriously and said, "That story wasn't an exaggeration or something I made up. That is exactly how I felt. That story is me."

I was shocked. I had known my brother in middle school, and to me, he was popular, funny, smart, and cool. I could not believe that this was how he had seen himself. I even asked him, "Are you sure your story did not go like this: You are the funny, popular guy. You make an appearance at the dance, plenty of girls want to dance with you, but you leave early with the guys at the punch bowl because the dance is lame to you. You are the leader, and everyone follows you out."

But that was not his story. He did not see himself the way I saw him. His feelings of insecurity and uncertainty shaped the narrative he had held onto for years. It was a reminder to me that the stories we tell ourselves, whether true or not, often come from our emotions, not reality. And sometimes, the way we feel about ourselves is vastly different from how others see us.

In a world where you constantly doubt yourself and never see your own true beauty, where you do not value who you are and believe you are undeserving, ask yourself: Who told you that? Who said you were ugly? Who said you had nothing more to offer? Often, it is not the world saying these things; it is us. If you do not believe in yourself, how are you going to accomplish anything?

My mom used to say, "Fake it till you make it. Only you know what you don't know." I remember the first time she said that, right after I graduated from hair school and got my first job. There was no teacher, no help, no one to guide me, just me walking into that salon on my own. But she was right. If I walked in confidently, without worrying about what service the client would ask for, I could make them feel comfortable. That client would believe in me, even if I did not believe in myself at the time.

Confidence is contagious. The more comfortable my clients felt, the more I started to believe in my own skills. The more I believed, the better I became. It was a lesson in how self-doubt can hold us back, while even a little bit of confidence can propel us forward. It is often those who feel the least capable who learn to project the most confidence.

So, what is stopping us from valuing ourselves? I have noticed that it is often other people's opinions that cloud our own sense of worth. Society likes to throw around the word "selfish" when we talk about caring for ourselves. But is valuing yourself really selfish? People often confuse self-value with neglecting others, as if focusing on your own needs means you are abandoning those around you. But in reality, self-value means recognizing your own needs and carving out space and time for yourself.

If you have worked hard, earned success, and done everything you can to reach your goals, shouldn't you be allowed to enjoy the fruits of your labor? The same goes for your time—you should be able to decide how you spend it, unapologetically.

The reason you do not do things for yourself is because deep down, you do not value yourself enough. It is not selfish to care for yourself, to put your energy into your own well-being. It is essential. When you value yourself, you show the world that you are worth something—and others will start to believe it too.

Finding your own worth is a lot like placing value on items. My mother-in-law is an expert at this. She's been doing estate sales for over 30 years, and most of the time, she's called in when someone has passed or is planning to move. Her job is to go through every item in a home and decide what it is worth. She has to know her stuff—whether something is original or a fake. She does her research, sometimes asking others for their opinion, and she has a sharp eye for what holds value, even if it is covered in dust or in need of a little polishing.

Now, imagine if you were in charge of placing value—not on items, but on yourself. Would you do the research to understand your own worth, or would you be quick to label yourself as a fake? Are you willing to let others decide your value for you, or are you ready to take ownership of it?

Just like those items at an estate sale, discovering your self-worth requires a bit of cleaning up and polishing. It is easy to overlook our own value when we are covered in the "dust" of self-doubt, past mistakes, or the opinions of others. But once we take the time to do the inner work, to uncover the real us underneath, we can see that we have always been worthy. We just needed to see ourselves clearly.

So, are you ready to place value on yourself, to recognize that you are authentic? Because no one else can set that price tag for you—it is up to you to realize just how much you are worth.

When I was in high school, I had a best friend. She was what I admired; she was smart. We spent most of our days together, sharing secrets, laughing, and dreaming of our future. But there was one secret I never shared with her—how I often felt like I was living in her shadow, only pretty on the outside and terribly stupid on the inside.

One afternoon, we were in class and the teacher told us we could pick our own partner. she, as always, took the lead and said we are partners.

I sat there, frozen, my mind a blank, I did not want to do a project with her. I felt a pang of inadequacy. In that moment, I was just the pretty sidekick in our friendship, unable to contribute anything meaningful. This feeling gnawed at me for days, slowly chipping away at my confidence.

A few days went by day at school; our teacher announced that we can work on our project now. My heart sank. As we began our project, I stared at the questions, feeling completely lost. My eyes wandered over to my best friend, who was writing furiously, a look of concentration on her face. I felt a wave of panic and embarrassment. I knew I would fail.

After school, we walked to our cars together in silence. She sensed something was wrong and asked, "What's up? You seem off today." I tried to brush it off, but she persisted. Finally, I blurted out, "I feel so stupid. I cannot even help with a simple project. I'm just...pretty."

My Best Friend stopped walking and looked at me with a mixture of confusion and concern. "What are you talking about? You are not stupid. Everyone has different strengths. You are amazing in your own way. Remember how you helped me organize and clean my whole room? I couldn't have done it without you."

Her words were kind, but they did not erase my feelings of inadequacy. I thanked her and changed the subject, not wanting to dwell on it any longer. That night, I lay in bed thinking about what she said. She was right—I did have my own strengths. But it was hard to shake the feeling that my identity was somehow stolen, that I was only seen as a pretty friend without much substance.

The next day, I decided to talk to my teacher Mrs. Huff about how I was feeling. To my surprise, she listened carefully and suggested we work together. We started meeting during school for extra help, and slowly, I began to understand the concepts that once seemed impossible. Mrs. Huff said I remind her a lot of herself I never asked her what that meant but she was a beautiful person, so I assumed she was a beautiful not smart student also. She always had so much grace for me. If I could see her now, I would say thank you and I know she would just know.

As weeks turned into months, I noticed a change in myself. I was not just the pretty girl anymore—I was becoming more confident in my abilities, both in and out of the classroom. We continued to be best friends, but now I felt like I was standing on equal ground. We supported each other, celebrated our differences, and embraced our unique talents. We graduated and went our separate ways.

Looking back, I realize that feeling inadequate was not about being stupid or pretty. It was about discovering who I was and recognizing my own worth. My identity was not stolen; it was just waiting to be uncovered. And once I found it, I knew I could be anything I wanted to be.

I genuinely believe that God places certain people in my life to help me grow and learn. Mrs. Huff and my best friend are prime examples of this divine intervention. Mrs. Huff, with her unwavering patience and wisdom, guided me through some of my toughest academic and personal challenges, always encouraging me to persevere and believe in myself. My best friend, with her steadfast loyalty and kindness, showed me the true meaning of friendship and support. Both of them, saved and living out their faith, have been instrumental in shaping who I am today, teaching me invaluable lessons about resilience, love, and the power of faith.

As I was growing up, I thought a lot about my doubts about God; during the many years of my childhood and how I truly felt about that, and not quite understanding even though I was being raised in a Christian and stable home why I would have these feelings. I knew though that I wanted what my parents had. These were some complicated and mixed-up feelings for a young girl, but in my heart of hearts I know now it was the holy spirit even though I did not understand that way back then growing up.

I have great memories of my whole life especially attending a Christian missionary alliance church. The Church was hugely involved in missions as we were always having a delightful crew of missionaries come to our church to enlighten us on the "wild stories" of how Jesus worked through them and healed the people they laid hands on. This was truly an amazing truth I came to believe and understand as the spirit moved me.

Fast forward to when I was 18 years old; I had the most wonderful opportunity offered to me to go to Ecuador. I was so vastly excited to join the group to help my fellow missionaries build a third story to a new church that they were erecting for their community. In my most pure thoughts I asked God if you are real, real to this world you created and you hear my plea, how could you not show me someone that would be healed. At that time in my life, I needed fulfilled in the strength of Jesus. I prayed and asked of our heavenly father to simply see a tumor the size of a watermelon shrink in front of my eyes.

When we finally arrived the noise and constant motion was a full-blown culture shock. One minute we were departing off the plane and the next minute it was a whirlwind of people swarming me. They were darting here and there wanting to help me, my gosh! I felt like Britney Spears, the singer where everyone thought I was a celebrity. In that moment I did feel like Britney Spears people were all over me after stepping off that plane. They were helping me with my luggage while smiling the whole time and helping me into the taxi to take us where we were going to stay in Ecuador. I was so anxious and excited at the same time!

When we arrived at our hotel in the city where we were to stay during our visit and after reaching our room, we had a long discussion on safety and why people behave this way. We understood it to be for money that they could earn because of the gut-wrenching poverty in many areas in that city. We were also warned of pick pocketers. We had several meetings throughout the day about our utmost safety and care, this really frightened me during our visit.

One of the missionary leaders that I met discussed with us about the people who lived there, she told us that a lot of these people hadn't even heard about God and had received no teaching or even knew there is a God, as well as what did God mean in their world?

We were fortunate and grateful that we had doctors that were joining us on this trip, they were going to set up a small open clinic for all people that needed health services but were unable to afford it. During the clinic there were so many people in need. We saw people and children with rashes, cuts, stomach aches, headaches, so many more ailments it was mind boggling and lo and behold day after day the lines got longer. It saddened us tremendously, although we came to realize this was a true blessing for these people to be able to have the care they needed.

Now on the third day we were there I was thinking about the prayer I sent up to Jesus… my own special prayer. I kept a remarkably close watch on people throughout these days to see if they had any tumors that I could see that were the size of a watermelon. I remember saying and praying God please show me.

Later, that day we all ended up making our way back to the hotel we were staying in to take much needed hot showers. After my shower as I was getting out of it to dry off, I had a severe pain somewhere around the middle of my stomach. I really ignored it as it was not too bad, I thought, so I continued with my day and went to lunch with everyone. Unfortunately, the stomach pain worsened and almost became unbearable, it felt like it had moved to the right side of my stomach, very quickly I suddenly doubled over with nausea and vomiting and was no longer able to walk. The leader of our group thought it was due to the food and that I had food poisoning. The leaders made a joint decision after seeing me in so much distress that they rushed me to the hospital to the emergency room. I was so shocked when we arrived in the emergency room as I was ushered into a waiting bed to see such very thin sheets with holes in them, everywhere you looked there was absolutely no privacy. To my distress and bewilderment, I thought to myself this looks like a war movie. In chronic pain and fear I prayed.

As the doctor arrived and checked me, he decided to do an imaging test on me because of my symptoms. I noticed while the test was being done that the abdominal ultrasound machine was incredibly old like the hospital room. He soon discovered an inflamed and swollen appendix. The doctor conveyed my diagnosis to the leaders that I was having an appendicitis and required that I undergo an emergency surgery before my appendix ruptured, it was imperative and needed to be removed immediately, he advised them that if they did the emergency surgery here at their hospital it would be a strong risk of infection and the Doctor didn't know if I could make it to fly back to the States before this occurred.

The missionaries in our whole group then gathered around me as I was lying in that bed in that hospital that day. I was by all accounts frightened, in pain and despondent. While they gathered around me as I was laying on there, they began to lay hands over me and my pain went away instantly! I knew immediately and without doubt that this was the watermelon tumor.

God used me in that hospital that day in front of everyone, even the doctor who saw, diagnosed me, and witnessed how swollen my belly was due to the appendicitis was in shock. I wanted to be alone when I got back from the hospital that day to willfully and agonizingly apologize to God and thank him for his true mercy and grace. I will never question God again.

A few months later after our trip to Ecuador, I remember thinking to myself and saying I would never question God again;

unfortunately, I found myself doing it again saying, "God I know you're a healer and that's what I questioned but why didn't you give me a brain that works?" Why didn't you make me smart?

I thought about this and how many years before I wanted to become a cosmetologist so bad and I was scared to take that test, luckily my mom encouraged me to take the test, while saying you got this! I remember her graciously giving me a Bible verse that said I can do all things through Christ who strengthened Philippians 4:13. I kept that verse with me the entire time I was in cosmetology school. This led me to think if I question God about healing and I know in my heart and soul that he is the number one healer, what would it hurt me to question him about why I am not smart?

I was talking to my mom one day about how I felt, she was with me in the salon that day getting her hair done and she said that the teacher had pulled her aside. She mentioned to her that I was the fastest, most efficient hairstylist finishing in half the time as the other stylists. She also said the other girls were thinking that this girl is naturally smart. It was then after having this conversation with my mother that I started to shift my focus to what smart really meant. To me smart did not mean that you knew the definition or pronounced every word correctly. Smart did not mean that you knew where every punctuation should be in a sentence. Smart did not mean that you could have the ability to write chapters and essays.

Shortly thereafter I started my fitness education right after completing cosmetology school, it was then that I realized that I did not have to know how to read or write my best to help someone with their health goals and teach them to become healthy and fit with my knowledge. I could lead them perfectly fine; I did not need to know any of this stuff to teach a fitness class to help someone get back into the best shape of their life.

My husband, a worship leader, has sung "The Father's House" by Cory Asbury countless times at church and during Celebrate Recovery. For context, Celebrate Recovery is a Christian 12-step program designed to help individuals overcome "hurts, hang-ups, and habits," grounded in principles from the Beatitudes. Even if one does not struggle with addiction, this program offers valuable support for navigating personal challenges.

One particular evening during a revival, as my husband sang this song; its lyrics resonated with me on a profound level. The song began with:

"Sometimes on this journey, I get lost in my mistakes. What looks to me like weakness is a canvas for your strength.

And my story isn't over, my story's just begun Failure won't define me cause that's what my father does."

In these words, I discovered a powerful truth: what I see as weakness can actually be an opportunity for growth and strength. For so long, I had struggled with feelings of inadequacy, particularly around my intelligence. The song's message—that failure does not define me and that my story is still unfolding—offered a much-needed perspective shift.

The lyrics continued to speak to me:

"Arrival's not the end game, the journeys where You are.

You never wanted perfect; you just wanted my heart."

This realization was transformative. My worth is not tied to perfection or intelligence but to my heart and my journey. The chorus—"A failure's never final when the father is in the room"—served as a reminder of the grace and renewal that faith offers. As the song progressed, it painted a vivid picture of transformation and hope:

"Prodigals come home.

The helpless find hope.

Love is on the move.

When the father's in the room."

These lines reinforced the idea that, regardless of our perceived shortcomings or failures, there is always room for redemption and growth when we embrace faith. The imagery of miracles and broken strongholds—"The Jericho walls are quaking' / Strongholds now are shaking'"—emphasized that change and healing are always within reach. The invitation to "lay your burdens down" and "check your shame at the door" underscored that we are accepted as we are, flaws and all.

In that moment, the song became my mirror for my own reflection. It showed me that my worth is not defined by external measures or past mistakes. Instead, it is rooted in the love and grace that are ever-present in the father's house. Even when I feel inadequate, I am still worthy of love and grace. The Father's house is a place where shame and failure are left behind, and where every part of our story—no matter how imperfect—is welcomed and transformed.

The Science of Beauty, Intelligence, and God's Design

Chapter 7

I have spent a lot of time pondering the "what ifs" and "what is" of life, especially when it comes to the power of appearances. In this book, I wanted to explore some of the research that validates many of the points I've personally experienced. One of the most striking examples that science provides us with is the undeniable truth that attractive people often benefit in life simply because of their looks. The question is, how much do we believe in these findings? I would guess that most of you reading this can think of times when you have witnessed this truth play out in your own unique circumstances of your life.

The research tells us that attractive individuals—those who fit societal standards of beauty—seem to glide through life with a smoother path than others. They qualify for better jobs, often leapfrogging over more experienced or skilled candidates. They receive higher pay and are invited to more social events, networking opportunities, and gatherings, simply because they "look the part." They even enjoy what seems like an overall higher quality of life.

I know this reality is not easy to swallow, especially for those who feel they do not meet this societal standard. It is hard not to wince at the unfairness of it all. But science has proven that people are hardwired to favor those who are attractive.

It is not just about finding them aesthetically pleasing. Our brains associate beauty with intelligence, competence, and even better health. This bias plays out across every area of life, from the workplace to personal relationships. We even make assumptions about the future success of attractive people's children. The world seems to be shaped by a bias that values appearance over substance, a truth many of us have seen firsthand.

Think about it: you cannot gauge someone's intelligence in the first few minutes of meeting them, but their looks can make an immediate and lasting impression. That initial reaction to beauty often shapes how we perceive their intellect and capability, even before they have spoken a word. Studies back this up—when we see someone who is attractive, our brains quickly assign them a range of other positive qualities. It is an almost automatic response, and while we may try to be objective, the truth is, it is nearly impossible to escape this bias.

But let us not forget that beauty, as much as it can open doors, can also bring its own set of challenges. Being attractive is not all smooth sailing. In fact, it can bring about a completely diverse set of problems—unwanted attention, envy, jealousy from peers, and even being objectified. People often reduce attractive individuals to their appearance, stripping them of their complexity as human beings. They forget that there is more to a person than the surface they see.

I have experienced this myself. When I was younger, the police stopped me several times—sometimes for minor traffic violations, sometimes for things I did not even realize were infractions. In each instance, I walked away with nothing more than a warning. Becky my assistant manager once joked, "It's because they saw your picture when they ran your plates and wanted to see a beautiful woman." I laughed it off at the time, but the more I thought about it, the more unsettling it became. Was my appearance really the reason I got off so easily? Would the same courtesy have been extended if I did not fit the conventional mold of beauty?

There was another situation that really drove this point home. I was at a friend's house with my boyfriend when the police arrived, responding to a noise complaint. Someone at the gathering quickly suggested, "Let Janie go talk to them—she'll charm them with her looks." That comment made me feel incredibly uncomfortable, not just because it reduced me to my appearance, but because it put me in a dangerous position. I later found out that drugs were in the house, and my friends could have been in serious trouble. It hit me hard that my appearance was being used as a tool to diffuse the situation. That moment made me realize that beauty, while powerful, could also be a weapon—sometimes one used against you.

These experiences brought me to an important realization. Science can tell us that attractive people benefit from something called the "attractiveness halo." It is this cognitive bias where we assume attractive individuals are smarter, more capable, and generally better than others. This bias shapes how we hire people, how we treat them socially, and even how we judge them in the legal system. You have seen this yourself—the attractive student who gets more attention from the teacher, the handsome guy who lands job interviews with ease, even if he is less qualified than others.

What is even more interesting is that researchers have found that attractiveness is often equated with good health. This perception even extends to the children of attractive people, who are believed to have an edge with their life before they have had a chance to prove themselves. It is a cycle that continues from generation to generation.

But as I have reflected on this, I have come to understand that science only scratches the surface. Appearances may shape how the world views us, but they do not define who we truly are. This is where faith steps in. While science highlights the privileges and biases associated with attractiveness, God's design goes far beyond physical beauty. In the eyes of the world, beauty can open doors, but in the eyes of God, it is our character, love, and wisdom that matter most.

While science may explain the benefits and biases that come with attractiveness, God's design goes beyond that. In the eyes of the world, beauty may open doors, but in the eyes of God, its character, love, and wisdom that truly matter. Scripture reminds us that "man looks at the outward appearance, but the Lord looks at the heart" (1 Samuel 16:7).

I have often reflected on how different the world might be if we valued people the way God does. If instead of focusing on the surface, we focused on the heart—on integrity, kindness, compassion, and strength of character. Beauty fades. Intelligence and wisdom grow. God has given each of us unique gifts, and those are the qualities that last.

Yes, science shows us that being attractive offers certain advantages, but it also reveals the limitations. Beauty may open doors, but it does not guarantee deep, meaningful relationships. It does not ensure peace of mind, nor does it eliminate life's challenges. In fact, it can sometimes create additional obstacles. The world may place attractiveness on a pedestal, but God's value system is infinitely deeper. He sees us for who we truly are, beneath the surface, and His love for us is not contingent on how we look.

As I have grown older, I have learned that real power comes from understanding our true value. It is not tied to our physical appearance but to who we are in Christ. As I reflect on my life, I have realized that the times I felt the most powerful were not when I looked my best, but when I acted with courage, integrity, and kindness. These are the moments that matter most. These are the qualities God values above all.

I remember starting my first real job at a high-end salon right after cosmetology school. It was a dream come true. The mirrors in the salon reflected success, confidence, and beauty, and I felt like

I was exactly where I was supposed to be. But it did not take long for me to notice something—people treated me differently because of how I looked. At first, I was flattered by the attention. Clients specifically asked for me, even though I was new and still learning. I told myself it was a good thing, but deep down, I started to wonder: Was it my skills they were interested in, or was it my appearance?

One afternoon, I was working on a client's hair, chatting casually as usual. She was a regular, and although she did not know me well, she started opening up about her life—her job, her family, her struggles. I listened, offering polite responses, until she stopped and looked at me in the mirror. Her gaze lingered, and then she said, "You must have an easy life, right? Look at you. A girl like you does not have to worry about much. You have beauty, a fantastic job, a boyfriend who adores you."

Her words hit me harder than I expected. She was not giving me a compliment—she was making assumptions about my life based on my looks. She had no idea that behind the polished exterior, I had struggled for years. She did not know that I had battled with reading comprehension, that I had felt inadequate and unintelligent for most of my school years. My looks may have opened doors, but they had not erased my struggles.

That experience stayed with me, and it made me question how people really saw me. Was I just a pretty face to them? Did my looks overshadow the demanding work, the late nights, and the effort I put into everything I did?

A few weeks later, something else happened that solidified this growing awareness. A high-profile client requested me specifically for a big event. As I worked on her hair, she studied me closely, and at one point, she said, "I heard you are the pretty one around here. That is why they gave you this job." Her words stung. All my dedication and effort seemed to vanish in an instant. To her, my appearance was the only reason I was there.

That is when I realized that beauty, while powerful, could also be limiting. It could open doors, but it could also obscure the depth of who I was. People saw what they wanted to see—a pretty face. They did not see the person behind it, the one who had struggled, worked hard, and fought to be where I was in life.

In the quiet moments that followed these experiences, I began to ask myself a different question: Who am I beyond my looks? That question marked the beginning of a journey, one that led me to focus less on how others saw me and more on how God saw me. I began to place less value on external validation and more on internal growth. Over time, I learned that my true worth was not in how I looked, but in the gifts, God had given me—gifts like kindness, creativity, and the ability to connect with others.

One day, I had a client who noticed the change in me. After I finished styling her hair, she looked at me with genuine warmth and said, "You know, there is something about you. It is not just your beauty—it is the way you make people feel. You have a gift, and it goes far beyond looks."

In that moment, I knew I had finally broken free from the narrative that had followed me for so long. Yes, I was attractive, but I was so much more than that. I had gifts that could not be captured in a mirror—gifts that God had placed in me, not to be hidden behind a pretty face but to be shared with the world.

This journey taught me that while society may place an enormous value on beauty, true worth comes from within. Beauty fades, but the person we become—the kindness we show, the love we give, the strength we build—those are the things that last. In the end, the world's standards of beauty are fleeting, but God's standard of who we are is eternal.

We live in a world that often values appearance over substance and shows the personal journey of realizing that true worth comes from within, and, from God's perspective. It brings the scientific bias toward beauty into personal context while tying it to a deeper truth about identity and value.

The Courage to Be Real: Conquering Impostor Syndrome

Chapter 8

In our quest to diagnose our challenges, impostor syndrome often emerges as a prevalent issue. Defined as a persistent fear of being exposed as a fraud despite evident accomplishments, it affects approximately 70% of individuals at some point in their lives. This psychological pattern, characterized by self-doubt and the belief that one is faking their success, can be particularly pronounced among high-achieving individuals. Interestingly, impostor syndrome tends to affect more female professionals, indicating that societal pressures and expectations might play a significant role.

For years, I grappled with impostor syndrome, continuously critiquing myself and replaying scenarios in my mind where I felt I fell short. I was my harshest critic, obsessing over perceived failures and shortcomings. This self-criticism seemed endless until a pivotal shift occurred in my perspective. I began to realize that striving for perfection was not only unrealistic but also counterproductive. This new understanding—that mistakes were not signs of failure but opportunities for growth—marked the beginning of my journey toward self-acceptance and authenticity.

One of the most challenging periods of my life was during my early career as a hairstylist. When I first embarked on this path, I was full of enthusiasm but plagued by self-doubt. Despite my training and passion, I often felt inadequate compared to my more experienced colleagues. I frequently questioned whether I had what it took to succeed in a field where appearance and skill seemed so crucial. It was during this time that my mother's advice—"fake it till you make it"—became my guiding mantra.

At first, the idea of "faking it" felt disingenuous. How could I be confident when I felt unsure of my skills? However, I soon realized that projecting confidence, even if it initially felt forced, could positively influence my interactions with clients. I began to approach each client with a newfound assurance, visualizing the desired outcome and channeling my inner belief that I could achieve it. Even when faced with techniques I had not fully mastered, I practiced improvisation with a smile and an air of confidence.

There were moments when the fear of being exposed as inexperienced or untalented—classic symptoms of impostor syndrome—crept in. Yet, each time these fears emerged, I reminded myself that feeling like an imposter was a normal part of the journey towards becoming a true professional. Over time, my clients started leaving the salon happier than ever and began requesting my services specifically. This positive feedback was a powerful testament to the impact of my newfound confidence. It became clear that the confidence I projected was not only beneficial to me but also reassuring to my clients, helping me grow into the skilled stylist I aspired to be.

Reflecting on those early years, I can now appreciate how much my mother's advice helped me. It was not about pretending to know everything; it was about having the courage to learn, adapt, and grow into my role as a hairstylist. This realization extended beyond hairstyling and influenced my approach to various aspects of my career and personal life. I started viewing my mistakes not as failures but as valuable lessons. Each misstep became a steppingstone, guiding me toward greater understanding and resilience.

One particular story stands out from my time working at the gym. I had always been a dedicated fitness enthusiast and, after becoming certified as a personal trainer, I managed the gym with passion and commitment. However, during one transition when the gym was sold, I faced numerous challenges. The change in ownership brought new expectations and pressures, and I felt a familiar pang of self-doubt. Yet, drawing on my previous experiences, I applied the same principles of confidence and adaptability. I approached each new challenge with the mindset that mistakes were part of the learning process, not indicators of failure. This approach helped me navigate the tumultuous period with greater ease and resilience.

Accepting imperfection was perhaps the hardest pill I had to swallow. I had always prided myself on delivering flawless work, but I came to understand that perfection is an illusion. Striving for excellence is admirable, but expecting flawless results is unrealistic and unnecessary. As I embraced my imperfections, I felt a weight lift off my shoulders—a sense of freedom and authenticity that I had never experienced before.

This shift in perspective allowed me to focus on continuous improvement rather than unattainable perfection. For many years, I grappled with a unique form of perfectionism. Unlike the typical perfectionist, who might set unachievable goals in their career or personal life, I made sure my objectives were always within reach, finding satisfaction in achieving them. However, this perfectionism revealed itself differently in my relationships, where my expectations were often unrealistic, leading to disappointment and strain.

This realization emerged during my time in the 12-step program, with the invaluable support of my sponsor, Jennifer. Through our discussions, I discovered how my perfectionist tendencies were impacting my relationships. I had imposed high standards that were challenging to meet, which led to frequent frustration and unmet expectations.

A transformative moment in this journey was understanding the biblical perspective on perfection. The verse from 2 Corinthians 12:9, where Paul writes, "My grace is sufficient for you, for my power is made perfect in weakness," struck a profound chord with me. It became clear that God's grace encompasses my imperfections and that His strength is magnified through my weaknesses.

This insight shifted my focus from striving for flawless relationships to pursuing spiritual maturity. I began to see my imperfections not as failures but as integral parts of my human experience. With the support of my sponsor and my growing faith, I learned to lean more on God's strength and grace rather than my own expectations.

As I let go of my perfectionistic tendencies, I discovered a deeper sense of peace and fulfillment in my relationships. I came to accept that mistakes and misunderstandings are natural components of any relationship, and growth often emerges from these very challenges. By focusing on developing virtues like humility, patience, and love, I aligned my actions more closely with God's teachings.

Through this transformative journey, I have experienced significant personal growth. The constant pressure to be perfect in my relationships has eased, replaced by a genuine appreciation for the journey of growth and the daily experience of God's grace. Embracing my imperfections has allowed me to build more authentic and meaningful connections, grounded in the understanding that God's love and grace are at work in every aspect of my life. May my story serve as a testament to the power of shifting from perfectionism to a focus on spiritual growth and self-compassion.

Self-compassion became a crucial component of my journey. I began to treat myself with kindness and understanding, much like I would a friend facing similar challenges. This compassionate approach enabled me to forgive myself for past mistakes and approach new challenges with optimism. Yet, the true breakthrough came during a meeting with my book editor Jamie. As we discussed my writing, my editor highlighted instances where I had shown genuine compassion towards others. This revelation was eye-opening, as I had always believed I lacked compassion.

Surprised by this feedback, I reflected on my life and recognized a pattern of self-criticism and harsh judgment. I recalled times when I berated myself for perceived failures and set impossibly ambitious standards. These habits had masked my ability to extend the same empathy and understanding to myself that I offered to others. Uncovering these ingrained beliefs, I embarked on a journey of forgiveness—releasing unrealistic expectations and embracing my imperfections as integral parts of my journey.

This process of self-forgiveness and acceptance has become a cornerstone of my personal growth. I have learned that self-compassion is not about excusing shortcomings but about acknowledging humanity's inherent flaws while nurturing a kinder inner dialogue. Each day, I am committed to practicing self-compassion, treating myself with the same patience and understanding I would extend to friends and family facing similar challenges.

As I continue to evolve, I am profoundly aware of God's unwavering presence and boundless compassion that has been my guiding light throughout this journey. His love envelops me, reminding me that I am never alone, even in the darkest moments of self-doubt. This divine presence has inspired me to cultivate a daily practice of self-compassion, to nurture a kinder inner dialogue, and to approach each day with a renewed sense of purpose and grace.

The journey through impostor syndrome has been one of deep introspection and personal growth. It has challenged me to confront my fears, to question the validity of my self-doubt, and to embrace the authenticity of my being. With each step, I have learned that true strength lies not in perfection but in the courage to be imperfectly human. This chapter stands as a testament to the transformative power of God's grace—a grace that has guided me through the murky waters of self-criticism and into the light of self-acceptance.

Embracing authenticity and overcoming impostor syndrome has not been a destination but a continuous journey. It is a daily commitment to recognize my worth, to forgive myself for past mistakes, and to believe in my capacity to grow and evolve. This journey has taught me that self-compassion is not a passive act but a powerful force that can reshape our lives. It allows us to heal from within, to build resilience, and to approach each challenge with a heart full of understanding and kindness.

My hope is that my reflections resonate with your heart and provide solace to those who, like me, have struggled with feelings of inadequacy and self-doubt. I pray that through these words, you find the courage to embrace the divine love that surrounds you—a love that begins with compassion for yourself and extends outward to others. May you find strength in the knowledge that you are worthy, not because of your achievements or perfection, but because of the inherent value bestowed upon you by a loving and compassionate God.

As you navigate your own journey, remember that every step toward self-compassion and authenticity is a step toward embracing the fullness of who you are. Allow yourself to be imperfect, to make mistakes, and to grow from them. In doing so, you honor the divine presence within you and radiate that love and compassion to the world around you.

In the end, it is this journey of embracing our true selves, grounded in God's love and grace that truly transforms our lives. It empowers us to overcome impostor syndrome, to rise above self-doubt, and to live with a heart open to both giving and receiving love. May you continue to evolve, guided by the light of divine compassion, and may your journey inspire others to find their own path to authenticity and self-worth.

Finding Purpose Beyond Doubts

Chapter 9

One spring afternoon, the scent of a clean linen candle wafted through the house, and as I sipped my tea, I could not shake the feeling of dissatisfaction that had been gnawing at me for weeks. Despite having a stable job at Coastal Finance, a place where I found fulfillment in serving others and going above and beyond in my role, there was an unsettling void within me—a sense that I needed to do more. Even though I excelled in my career and made a meaningful impact, there was a persistent feeling that something was missing, a deeper calling or a broader purpose that extended beyond the confines of my professional life.

The question "What is my purpose?" had become a constant companion, whispering doubts and insecurities into my mind. I felt stuck in a cycle of routine and uncertainty, as if I were navigating life on autopilot. My days were filled with responsibilities and commitments, but I often wondered if I was merely going through the motions without a clear sense of direction or meaning. The satisfaction I derived from my work at Coastal Finance was genuine, but it felt as though there was a deeper layer of purpose I was missing.

I frequently found myself reflecting on whether my daily actions were aligned with a higher calling or if they simply fulfilled immediate needs. Was I truly making a difference, or was I just adding to the noise of everyday life? Despite my efforts to excel and serve in my role, the nagging feeling that there was more I was meant to do persisted.

This sense of restlessness grew more pronounced with time, leading me to question if there was a greater purpose waiting to be discovered. I began to seek answers beyond the tangible successes and achievements of my career. I longed for a deeper connection to something greater, a sense of fulfillment that transcended professional accomplishments.

In an effort to explore this longing, I started to look beyond my routine and delve into personal reflection and spiritual inquiry. I sought out ways to connect more profoundly with my faith and to understand how my gifts and talents could be used in a broader context. I engaged in meaningful conversations.

Through these explorations, I began to recognize that my quest for purpose was not just about achieving more or taking on new projects but about aligning my life with a deeper sense of meaning and connection. I discovered that purpose often lies in the intersection of personal passions, spiritual insights, and the impact we have on others.

One evening, overwhelmed by these feelings, I decided to take a walk, hoping that a change of scenery might help clear my mind. As I gazed at the beauty of the natural world around me, my thoughts turned inward. I began to reflect on my faith and how God's presence had been a constant in my life, even when I felt lost. I recalled verses from Scripture that spoke of God's guidance and purpose, such as Proverbs 3:5-6 (NIV): "Trust in the Lord with all your heart and lean not on your own understanding; in all your ways submit to Him, and He will make your paths straight."

It was then that I realized I had been searching for purpose in all the wrong places. I had been expecting a grand, dramatic revelation, when in reality, purpose often unfolds in the everyday moments of life, guided by God's hand. If you know me, I am a "go big or go home" type of person. My doubts had clouded the simple truth that purpose is not always about a single, monumental achievement. Instead, it is about finding meaning and fulfillment in the small, daily acts of love, service, and creativity.

I returned home with a renewed sense of clarity. I picked up my journal and began to write down the insights I had gained. I acknowledged that my purpose could be found in the simple acts of kindness I extended to others, the creativity I nurtured, and the way I chose to live each day with intention and love, trusting that God had a plan for me in all of it.

In the weeks that followed, I began to embrace this newfound understanding of purpose. I began volunteering at the Rose House, as a source of joy and fulfillment, believing that God was working through me to touch others' lives. I focused on being present in my relationships, valuing the moments of connection and support that enriched my life, recognizing that these were ways God was using me to love and serve others.

I also discovered a deep passion for guiding women and youth. Through my nonprofit, Lit, and The Lit Show, I have been able to reach multiple women and support them through their daily struggles. It became clear to me that God has surrounded me with a community of strong, supportive individuals who have been instrumental in helping me understand and embrace my purpose. These people have spoken into my life with wisdom and encouragement, providing the strength and clarity I needed to fully release and pursue the purpose that God has set before me. Their presence and influence have been pivotal in shaping my journey, demonstrating that purpose is often revealed through the support and guidance of those who genuinely care and believe in our potential.

Through this journey, I discovered that purpose is not always about grand, visible successes but about the quiet, everyday ways we contribute to the world and find joy in our passions. My doubts began to fade as I embraced the truth that purpose is often found in the simplest, most sincere expressions of love and creativity, guided by God's wisdom and grace.

I wrestled with a question that seemed to shadow every achievement and failure: Why wasn't I as smart? Why did my brain feel like a constant source of frustration? In a family where academic excellence and quick wit were celebrated, my slow processing and difficulties in keeping up with others often left me feeling like an outsider.

In school, while my sister excelled with a swift grasp of concepts and quick completion of assignments, I struggled to keep pace. Every time she was praised for her brilliance, a knot of insecurity tightened in my chest. I know it was the enemy and I would wonder why God had not endowed me with a mind like hers. Why did I have to labor so hard for results that seemed to come naturally to others? These questions began to erode my faith, planting seeds of doubt about whether God truly saw me, whether He had a purpose for me, and whether He genuinely cared about my struggles.

As the years passed, these doubts intensified. It felt as though my intellectual limitations were a cruel joke played by a God who had designed me to be less capable, less intelligent than those around me. I questioned why God had not made me smarter, why He had created me with such difficulties, and why I constantly felt like I was lagging.

One evening, as I sat alone in my room, grappling with profound and unanswered questions, I reached for my Bible. I opened it to Ephesians 2:10 (NIV): "For we are God's handiwork, created in Christ Jesus to do good works, which God prepared in advance for us to do." I clung to these words, hoping they would reassure me of God's unique purpose for each of us. Although the verse spoke of God's intricate design and purposeful creation, it did not fully dispel the doubts that had taken root in my heart.

However, through ongoing reflection and prayer, I began to uncover a new dimension of God's love and purpose. I realized that my struggles were not a reflection of God's neglect but rather an opportunity for growth. My difficulties with learning and processing information had shaped me in ways I had not fully grasped. They had taught me patience, perseverance, and empathy—qualities that I might not have developed otherwise. I began to see that God had not made a mistake in creating me as I am; instead, He had a purpose in mind, one that involved using my unique experiences and challenges to grow and help others.

Slowly, my perspective began to shift. I started to appreciate how my struggles had forged a deeper connection with others who faced similar challenges. My journey through doubt and self-discovery became a testament to the fact that God uses our weaknesses and struggles to build something meaningful. I began to understand that my value was not determined by how quickly I learned or how easily I grasped concepts but by the love and purpose God had instilled in me from the beginning.

In conversations with friends, family, and mentors, I found wisdom. They reminded me that everyone has their own path to walk, and that God's love is not limited by our perceived strengths or weaknesses. Through these interactions and my journey of faith, I came to understand that God's creation of me was perfect in its own way. My intellectual challenges did not diminish my worth or potential; instead, they highlighted the need for trust and faith in a plan greater than my immediate understanding.

I learned that God's plan for each of us is woven with threads of grace and purpose, even when the tapestry seems unclear. My doubts began to transform into a deeper faith, one that acknowledged that God's ways are not always our ways, and His wisdom surpasses our understanding. My journey was not just about finding answers but about learning to trust in a God who sees the full picture, even when we can only see a small part of it.

And so, as I looked out the window one spring afternoon, I felt a profound sense of peace. I had found a purpose that resonated deeply with my heart—one that transcended doubts and celebrated the beauty of the ordinary moments that make life truly meaningful, knowing that God was with me every step of the way.

Taking the Reins: Owning My Actions and Reactions

Chapter 10

When I accepted the manager position, I noticed "GIRL BOSS" imagery everywhere, almost like when you buy a new car and suddenly see that model on every street. It is fascinating how once you focus on something; it seems to manifest all around you. This phenomenon was not just a coincidence; it was a reflection of how our minds work.

One day, my car dealer Tim came into my office and saw some of my "GIRL BOSS" decorations. He complimented them, and this gave me an opportunity to share what "GIRL BOSS" means to me. I explained to him that for me, "GIRL BOSS" is not merely about being a woman in charge—it is about being in control of myself. I told him, "I am the boss of me, 'GIRL BOSS' means I am taking the reins: I own my actions and reactions. It's about how I manage myself and the situations that come my way."

Tim is the epitome of taking the Reins. As a remarkable businessperson, he exemplifies integrity by taking responsibility for his decisions and responses. Leading 1st Choice Auto Sales, Tim goes beyond expectations to ensure customer satisfaction. His commitment to excellence is evident in how he rectifies mistakes promptly and strives to surpass customer expectations. Tim's approach underscores his dedication to both his business and principles, making him a standout example of leadership in action.

This perspective is rooted in a lesson my mom always emphasized. She would say, "You train people in how to treat you." It took me a long time to fully understand this concept, but over the years, I came to realize that we are responsible for setting the boundaries of what we accept in our lives.

If you permit someone to raise their voice at you without facing any consequences, they will continue to do so. If you tolerate name-calling, others will believe it is acceptable behavior. What you tolerate not only affects how others perceive you but also influences who you become. It is crucial to recognize that our tolerance sets the stage for how we are treated and how we respond to those treatments.

From the moment we are born, our parents guide us to respect authority. In our homes, parents play the role of authority figures, teaching us how to behave—how to sit, eat, use manners, and care for ourselves. They establish routines and teach us the value of punctuality and adherence to schedules. This preparation is designed to equip us for the day when we will need to take control of our own lives.

However, not everyone grows up with such guidance. Some may feel they were not given the tools necessary to navigate adulthood successfully. But the good news is that you can give yourself these tools. You have the power to take responsibility for who you are and decide what you will and will not accept in your life. It is about taking charge and setting standards for how you expect to be treated.

In the professional world, especially in my line of work, people can be incredibly harsh. Rumors spread quickly, especially when things are not going well or when financial issues arise. People are often quick to blame others rather than accepting responsibility for their own actions. In the past, I found myself becoming a target of such negativity because I allowed it. I recognized that if I permitted people to think it was okay to act in ways that could harm me or my business, I was only hurting myself. I was relinquishing control and, in doing so, letting myself down.

One of the most important lessons I have learned as an adult is the power of letting go. Not every battle is worth fighting; not every argument needs to be won. I have come to understand that maintaining control often means choosing when to let go. Even if I allow someone else to have the last word, I am still in control. Realizing that being right is not always the ultimate goal has been liberating.

Taking control of how you view yourself is equally essential. We can be our own harshest critics. If you continuously berate yourself, you will find it challenging to move forward. It is like trying to walk while someone keeps tripping you—and that someone is you. To effectively teach others how to treat you, you must first learn to treat yourself with respect and kindness.

The idea of being in charge of yourself extends beyond managing your reactions; it involves allowing your inner beauty to shine through. This goes beyond physical appearance—it is about how you carry yourself, how you think, and how you interact with the world. When you cultivate a powerful sense of self-respect and self-worth, others will notice and treat you accordingly.

Embarking on this journey of self-management, of being your own boss, is not always straightforward. It demands constant reflection, a willingness to grow, and an unwavering commitment to your values. It involves recognizing your worth, setting boundaries, and standing firm in your beliefs. It is about knowing when to let go and when to stand your ground. Most importantly, it is about understanding that you are in control of your life and destiny. The reins are in your hands, and it is up to you to steer them toward the life you desire.

Before I truly got to know the CEO (then) of my company, I observed something that left a profound impact on me. He was not the type of leader who merely sat behind a desk, issuing commands. Instead, he led by example. When he walked into the office, he did not just inspect the space from a distance or delegate mundane tasks to others. If he noticed that the paper shredder was overflowing, he would oversee it himself. If the carpet needed vacuuming, he would grab the vacuum and get the job done.

One day, I saw him taking care of these tasks, and I offered to help, saying, "I can do that." He looked at me and said something that resonated deeply: "How do you expect me to tell you to do it if I won't do it myself?" His simple words carried a powerful message about leadership and responsibility. That day, I made a mental note of his philosophy, as it encapsulated the kind of leadership approach I aspired to adopt in my own career.

This experience taught me that true leadership goes beyond merely directing others; it involves rolling up your sleeves and collaborating with your team. It is easy to delegate tasks and tell others what needs to be done, but authentic leadership requires humility and a willingness to engage at every level of the job. When you demonstrate that you are not above performing the tasks you might usually delegate, you earn respect and foster trust within your team.

Starting from the bottom myself, I have always embraced the value of demanding work. I do not shy away from tasks that might seem minor or routine because I recognize that every effort contributes to the larger goal. Whether it involves cleaning up a workspace, addressing customer complaints, or managing intricate details of a project, I am ready to dive in. This direct approach not only keeps me grounded but also sets a standard for those around me. When your team sees that you are willing to put in the arduous work, they are more inclined to mirror that dedication.

This leadership philosophy is about more than just completing tasks; it is about fostering an environment where every contribution is valued, regardless of size. It underscores that leadership is a service, not a privilege, and that being in charge means taking responsibility for every aspect of the work, not just the more glamorous or visible parts.

Such an approach has significantly influenced how I interact with colleagues and the expectations I set for myself. I have learned that leading by example is one of the most effective ways to inspire and motivate others. It is not sufficient to merely speak the right words; your actions must align with those words. By demonstrating consistency between what you say and what you do, you build credibility and cultivate a culture of mutual respect and collaboration.

Being in charge is not about wielding power or authority; it is about embodying accountability and integrity. It means showing up every day prepared to support your team and achieve collective goals. It is about understanding that true leadership is reflected in action, not just in verbal instructions.

When I first started working in the office, someone remarked that it was not my physical appearance that impressed him, but rather what was beneath the surface. This comment made me reflect on the metaphor of a mask—one that people often use to conceal their insecurities and feelings of inadequacy. Many individuals remain in their comfort zones, hesitant to apply for positions or seize opportunities due to self-doubt about their appearance or perceived lack of worth.

I have observed numerous people shy away from opportunities because they underestimate their own value, mistakenly believing their worth is tied solely to their physical appearance. In truth, genuine value emanates from within—often hidden talents or skills that may not be immediately apparent to others.

A pivotal moment for me came when I first felt truly valued in my company, and it had nothing to do with my looks. This occurred while managing insurance claims over the phone, where my appearance was irrelevant. Despite this, I successfully recovered thousands of dollars for a total loss claim. At the time, I did not fully understand the nuances of negotiating settlement amounts. When the company owner said, "We're not accepting that amount," I was initially surprised. I thought the offer seemed fair based on the car's value and assumed the owner had significant power.

The owner patiently explained that people sometimes make offers without fully comprehending the true value of what they are negotiating. They might undervalue an item because they are unaware of its complete worth or additional features. This experience highlighted that people often settle for less because they do not fully appreciate the hidden potential or additional value that an item—or a person—can offer.

Reflecting on this lesson in my personal life, I realized that many people, including myself, might not fully recognize their unique qualities or additional attributes. It is like the difference between a custom-built car and a standard model. Just as a custom-built car has unique features and enhancements that set it apart, I too possess qualities that go beyond the surface. I am like a custom creation with value that transcends mere appearance. It is up to me to recognize and assert this inherent worth.

The insights I gained from that experience have profoundly influenced my approach to self-worth and personal growth over the past eight years. They have reinforced the understanding that my true value is not confined to what is immediately visible but encompasses a deeper, more meaningful essence.

My mom always used to say, "You never get a second chance to make a first impression." Her advice went beyond just being careful with my words and actions; it was a reminder to present myself with grace and class from the very start.

I have made it a point to keep this saying prominently displayed in my office. It serves as a visible reminder for my customers, my employees, and for me personally. I can always control how I treat others and the respect I show them.

Growing up, I learned that while you cannot control other people's thoughts and feelings, you should not let their opinions hold you back.

One vivid memory from my childhood underscores this lesson. In my early school years, I was heavily involved in various fundraisers. My sales journey began in kindergarten. This success sparked a range of reactions from my classmates. For instance, during a dog food drive, I brought in a considerable amount of donations. Some of my classmates were impressed and thought it was cool, but others felt envious. Regardless of the reactions I faced, I knew that I would not stop pursuing my goals just because someone did not want me to be successful.

These early experiences taught me valuable lessons about competition and the varied reactions it can provoke. They showed me that while others may have their opinions, what truly matters is how I present myself and treat those around me. I have learned that my worth is not defined by external validation but by my actions and the respect I extend to others.

My dad, one of twelve siblings, often reminisced about his childhood when food was a precious commodity they had to stretch carefully. He vividly recalled times when their meals were as simple as bread and butter, emphasizing how they made every penny count. These early experiences instilled in him a profound appreciation for abundance, which he celebrated with enthusiasm at every holiday and family gathering.

Family gatherings on his side were a sensory feast, overflowing with homemade delights. The table was brimming with a variety of treats, from cookies and candies to hearty meals like meatballs, spaghetti, and sausages. Each dish was steeped in tradition, with recipes handed down through generations, carrying stories and memories.

On my mom's side, while family meals and celebrations were equally cherished, there was a different focus. My mom was a staunch advocate for healthier eating habits. She emphasized balanced nutrition, encouraging us to opt for fruits over sweets and to be mindful of portion sizes. Her approach was motivated by a desire to maintain good health and prevent weight gain, reflecting her love and concern for our well-being.

Despite their differing approaches, both sides of my family shared a common thread: food was more than just sustenance. It was a way to express love, preserve traditions, and create lasting memories.

When I was thirteen, I began working at the gym where my sister taught workout classes. This early exposure to fitness set the tone for my life. By twenty, I was certified in aerobics and personal training, managed a gym, and maintained a healthy weight by following a low-carb diet and a rigorous workout routine.

However, in 2021, my journey took an unexpected turn when I became pregnant. At my 8-week checkup, I learned I had a blood clot between the placenta and uterine wall, which put me on pelvic rest and prevented me from working out. Used to a strict low-carb diet, I began eating bread with peanut butter to ease nausea, which, combined with my inactivity, led to significant weight gain. By the time I went into labor at 37 weeks, I had gained almost eighty pounds.

Throughout my pregnancy, my family, friends, and church community were incredible prayer warriors, supporting me in every way. My friend Carmen was particularly supportive, sending me prayers and encouragement every step of the way. After a complicated delivery and surgery to remove the placenta, I faced a tough recovery, including a blood transfusion and months of low energy while caring for my newborn.

Although I struggled to lose weight while breastfeeding, my doctor reminded me that everyone's postpartum journey is different. It took time, but gradually I regained my energy.

This experience brought me a profound understanding of the challenges related to weight and fitness, something I had not fully grasped before. My friend Jennifer encouraged me to start a workout group where we could support one another and empower other women. After much prayer and discussion with my brother Josh—who was already involved in a faith-based workout program—I felt inspired to create something even bigger: a nonprofit organization. Ladies In Transformation (L.I.T) was born in April 2023.

I have been deeply impressed by the number of women who have stepped up to make a difference. Becky, our resolute fitness director, has been with me every step of the way on my fitness journey. Her selflessness and genuine care for women have been invaluable.

Our mission at L.I.T is to uplift and empower women from all backgrounds, fostering transformative change in their physical, social, mental, and spiritual dimensions. In April 2024, Britt—my best friend and the president of L.I.T—and I proudly launched the L.I.T Show podcast to further our reach and emphasize the social aspect of our mission. You can check out our podcast at <u>The L.I.T Show</u>. Supporting and serving women in these holistic ways feels like a divine calling, and I am deeply passionate about this work.

Now, with a unique perspective on health and fitness, I am determined to take control of my actions and reactions. I have learned that true strength comes from within, and it is not just about physical fitness—it is about mental and emotional resilience too. I am committed to helping other women on their transformation journeys, focusing not just on weight loss but on transforming the mind, body, and spirit.

By taking the reins of my life, I have realized the importance of self-love, set boundaries, and embracing challenges as opportunities for growth. I am now driven to empower other women to do the same, turning their struggles into strength and helping them to own their actions and reactions, just as I have learned to do.

The Price of Knowing: Eve's Story and the Struggle for Understanding

Chapter 12

Eve possessed a mind unlike any other—a mind that saw the world not just as it was but as it could be, through a lens of infinite possibilities, subtle mysteries, and a boundless capacity for empathy. This unique way of thinking was both a blessing and a challenge. It was her gift, allowing her to perceive beauty and complexity in ways others could not, but it was also the source of her greatest internal conflict. Her deep thirst for understanding and knowledge made her stand out, shaping her into a figure of exceptional wisdom, but it also led her into the profound dilemma that would forever alter the course of humanity.

Eve lived in the Garden of Eden, a place of unparalleled beauty and serenity. The garden was alive with vibrant colors, intoxicating fragrances, and creatures that harmonized with nature in perfect symphony. Each tree and flower seemed to sing with the breath of life, a reflection of God's perfect creation. Yet, amid all this perfection, one tree stood apart—the Tree of Knowledge of Good and Evil. Its fruit gleamed, not just with beauty, but with a silent promise. It whispered deeper truths, secrets of the universe, the essence of good and evil itself.

As Eve walked through the garden one day, she found herself drawn to the tree. There was something irresistible about it, an invisible pull that went beyond mere curiosity. It was not just the allure of the forbidden; it was her mind—her innate desire to understand the world more fully—that drew her in. Eve had always been wired for more. She did not just want to see the world in its superficial beauty; she wanted to dive deeper, to uncover the layers of wisdom hidden beneath the surface. It was in her nature to seek meaning, to question, to grow.

The serpent, sensing her internal struggle, approached her with calculated precision. "Eve," it whispered, its voice smooth and enticing, "have you ever wondered why you are forbidden from this knowledge? What if I told you that this fruit holds the answers to everything you have ever wanted to understand? One bite, and you will see the world for what it truly is—all its truths laid bare before you."

Eve paused, her mind racing. She knew the command: they were not to eat from this tree. But the serpent's words resonated with her. Knowledge. Understanding. She had always felt an insatiable hunger for these things, a desire to be more, to know more. What would it be like to comprehend the very fabric of existence? To understand the delicate dance between good and evil, between light and dark? Her soul longed for it.

"For the Lord gives wisdom; from His mouth comes knowledge and understanding" (Proverbs 2:6). This verse could have echoed in Eve's spirit, had she remembered that wisdom comes from God and not from the serpent's empty promises.

With trembling hands, driven by this deep, unquenchable thirst for wisdom, Eve reached for the fruit. She held it for a moment, feeling the weight of the decision before bringing it to her lips. As she took a bite, the world around her seemed to shift. The moment the juice touched her tongue, her mind was flooded with revelations. She saw the complexities of the human condition, the interplay of joy and suffering, the consequences of her choice. She understood the enormity of what she had done and the cascade of events that would follow.

From the very beginning, Eve's struggle feels achingly familiar, as though her ancient story echoes in the hearts of so many women today. In a world where beauty often overshadows intellect, Eve stood as the first to feel the pangs of wanting to be more than what she appeared to be. Imagine her, created with divine perfection, her long hair cascading down her shoulders, her flawless skin glowing under the sun. She was physically perfect—crafted by God's own hands—but still, that was not enough for her.

What was Eve really craving in that moment by the tree? It was not just the taste of forbidden fruit. It was the allure of knowledge, of wisdom, of being able to grasp something more profound. She longed for the kind of understanding that she believed would make her truly complete. It was not her body or her beauty that she doubted—it was her mind. Perhaps she wondered if her beauty was all that defined her, and so she reached for more, hoping that knowledge would fill the gap.

In that fateful moment, Eve became the embodiment of the tension that so many feel: the struggle between the outward appearance and the inner self. She, like others, wanted to prove that she was not just a pretty face—that she had depth, that she could understand the mysteries of the universe. It is as if, even in the Garden of Eden, Eve felt unseen, unheard. Her outward beauty could not satisfy the deeper longing to be valued for something greater.

The tragedy in Eve's story is that she already was enough. She already possessed the fullness of everything God had designed for her to be. But the serpent's whisper planted doubt, the same kind of doubt that so many experience today. The lie that who we are is not enough, that we must reach for something external to validate our worth. Eve's mistake was not in her pursuit of knowledge but in believing that she lacked anything in the first place.

Eve's desire to be known for more than her beauty speaks to the deeper human condition: the quest for significance beyond what others can see. And her story, though tragic, is a reminder that even in our imperfections and insecurities, we are already made complete by God. Her craving for wisdom may have led to her downfall, but it also highlights a universal truth—the longing to be valued for who we truly are, inside and out. And in that truth, we can find grace.

And in a multitude of ways, I see myself in her story. Just like Eve, the enemy placed a label on me, trying to convince me that I was not smart enough, that I was not capable of understanding, that I was only valued for what I looked like on the outside. That voice of doubt has echoed in my mind so many times, telling me that I am not enough—that I will never be enough. "The thief comes only to steal and kill and destroy; I have come that they may have life and have it to the full" (John 10:10). The enemy tried to steal Eve's sense of identity and purpose, just as he had tried with me. But Jesus came to give me life in all its fullness, reminding me that I am enough.

I recall a particular instance during high school when preparing for my driver's ed test, which resonated deeply with the story of Eve in the Garden of Eden. The pressure to perform well was immense, and despite my best efforts to study and prepare, I felt unprepared and overwhelmed by the thought of failure.

As the test approached, a classmate who seemed confident and well-prepared offered me a way out. They had a set of notes and answers for the driving test and suggested I use them. The temptation was strong—much like Eve was enticed by the forbidden fruit, I was drawn to the promise of an easy solution that seemed to guarantee a passing grade.

The idea of cheating felt like a quick fix. I imagined the relief of passing the test effortlessly and the pride of receiving my driving license. The thought of avoiding stress and potential failure was incredibly appealing.

Despite knowing that cheating conflicted with my values, I decided to go through with it. During the test, I discreetly used the notes and passed with flying colors. At first, I felt a rush of accomplishment, but as time passed, I was unable to shake the feeling of guilt and unease.

Reflecting on the situation, I realized how much it mirrored Eve's experience. Just as Eve was tempted by the allure of the forbidden fruit, I was tempted by the promise of an easy path to success. While the immediate result was gratifying, the long-term effects were more complex. I grappled with the knowledge that I had compromised my integrity and failed to earn my achievement honestly.

This experience taught me a profound lesson about the importance of staying true to my values, even when faced with temptation. Just as Eve's choice had far-reaching consequences, my decision to cheat had a lasting impact on my sense of self-respect and integrity. It was a powerful reminder that true success and fulfillment come from hard work and honesty, not shortcuts and deceit.

I know that God sees me differently not as a cheater. He has made me smart enough to fulfill His plans and purpose for my life. As Jeremiah 29:11 says, "For I know the plans I have for you," declares the Lord, "plans to prosper you and not to harm you, plans to give you hope and a future." His plan for me is greater than the doubts and lies that the world or even my own mind can plant. This verse reassures me that God's plan is far more significant than any temptation I may face. I know that God sees me differently. He has made me smart enough to fulfill His plans and purpose for my life. His plan for me is greater than the doubts and lies that the world, or even my own mind, can plant.

That does not mean everything comes easily to me. I must work hard, I must study, and I must put in the effort to learn. It does not come naturally, but what I have realized is that I am not doing it alone. "I can do all this through Him who gives me strength" (Philippians 4:13). When I pray, when I focus on God's promises, I know that He will never leave me or forsake me. "Be strong and courageous. Do not be afraid; do not be discouraged, for the Lord your God will be with you wherever you go" (Joshua 1:9). This verse has been my anchor, reminding me that I am never alone in my journey toward wisdom and growth.

I was created by God, designed by Him with intention, and defined by His love. "For we are God's handiwork, created in Christ Jesus to do good works, which God prepared in advance for us to do" (Ephesians 2:10). I have everything I need—every ounce of wisdom and intelligence to grow, to learn, and to fulfill my purpose.

God has equipped me with a brain capable of learning and wisdom. "If any of you lacks wisdom, you should ask God, who gives generously to all without finding fault, and it will be given to you" (James 1:5). I may not always feel like the smartest person in the room, but I trust that I am enough because I am His creation. I have the mental capacity, the drive, and the resources to grow in knowledge. When I lean on Him and allow His strength to guide me, I am reminded that my worth isn't found in the labels the world tries to place on me, but in the truth of who God says I am—capable, intelligent, and enough just as I am.

On this journey of self-discovery, I have come to understand that true wisdom does not require being the smartest. Wisdom is found in humility, in the willingness to learn, to grow, and to seek guidance from the One who knows all. It is about trusting that I am enough—not because I have earned it, not because I look a certain way, and not because I have all the answers—but because I am His creation, fearfully and wonderfully made. "I praise You because I am fearfully and wonderfully made; Your works are wonderful; I know that full well" (Psalm 139:14). I am not defined by my achievements, my outward appearance, or the expectations others place upon me. I am defined by the love of my Creator, who knit me together with purpose and intention.

Through every challenge, every moment of doubt, and every time the world has tried to tell me that being pretty or outwardly perfect is what matters most, I have learned that true strength and true wisdom come from something deeper. They come from within—from the spirit God placed inside me, from the heart that He has shaped over time, and from the lessons I have learned in both failure and success. "But the Lord said to Samuel, 'Do not consider his appearance or his height, for I have rejected him. The Lord does not look at the things people look at. People look at the outward appearance, but the Lord looks at the heart'" (1 Samuel 16:7). My worth is not measured by worldly standards of beauty or intelligence, but by the depth of my character and the love that I carry for others.

There have been moments when I have felt the pressure to be more—to be smarter, to look better, to prove myself in ways that would make me seem "enough" in the eyes of others. But the truth is, I do not need to prove anything. I have the mental capacity, the drive, and the resources to grow in knowledge and wisdom, and I am not on this journey alone. When I lean on God, when I let His strength guide me, I am reminded daily that He is my source. He is the one who fills the gaps in my understanding, who strengthens me when I am weak, and who reveals my true worth when I feel diminished. "But He said to me, 'My grace is sufficient for you, for my power is made perfect in weakness.' Therefore, I will boast more gladly about my weaknesses, so that Christ's power may rest on me" (2 Corinthians 12:9).

I have learned that beauty fades, intelligence grows, and strength is forged in the fire of life's challenges. But through it all, I remain steadfast in the truth that my worth has never wavered in God's eyes. In a world that often values appearance over substance, I have found peace in knowing that God values the heart and the mind He gave me. He sees beyond the surface and calls me to live in the fullness of who I am, embracing both my strengths and my imperfections with grace.

As I close this chapter of my journey, I hold fast to this truth: it is not always smart to be pretty. The world may celebrate outward beauty, but it is the beauty of the mind, the beauty of wisdom, and the beauty of a heart aligned with God's will that truly lasts. I am learning to be content with the gifts I have been given, knowing that I am equipped for every excellent work He has planned for me. I am capable. I am intelligent. And I am enough—just as I am.

So, to the one reading this, whether you feel the weight of expectations, the pressure to look a certain way or be a certain way, know this: You are enough, exactly as God made you. You do not have to be the prettiest or the smartest by the world's standards, because God has already declared you valuable. You are capable of greatness, of wisdom, and of love that transforms lives, starting with your own. "For we are God's handiwork, created in Christ Jesus to do good works, which God prepared in advance for us to do" (Ephesians 2:10). Let that truth guide you, let it free you, and let it remind you that you are so much more than what you see in the mirror. You reflect the divine, wonderfully made, and always enough.

The Mirror and the Mind: Uncovering True Self Worth

Chapter 12

Authoring this book has stirred up a lot of past pain for me. It is one thing to think you are not smart, but it is another to confront those feelings head-on and put them down on paper. Throughout my school years, I often felt like I was reflecting a version of myself that did not align with who I genuinely wanted to be. My struggles with reading and learning seemed like a mirror that distorted my self-image, showing a reflection of inadequacy rather than potential.

In eighth grade, we were assigned *Where the Red Fern Grows*. Since our family did not watch much TV, we had a collection of Focus on the Family movies, and this film was among them. Instead of reading the book, I watched the movie. This was a recurring pattern for me—if I could not avoid reading, I would ask my sister to summarize books like *To Kill a Mockingbird*, knowing she had read everything available. My efforts to avoid reading were a way to cope with the pain of feeling like I did not measure up.

It is embarrassing to admit, but my struggles with reading were so profound that I did not truly grasp it until my second attempt in eighth grade. Each chapter I managed to read on my own felt like a huge victory but learning always felt like a struggle rather than something enjoyable. It was as though my reflection in the mirror showed me as someone who was not smart, and no amount of effort seemed to change that image.

During my senior year, another significant challenge arose: the senior project, which was crucial for my graduation. Overwhelmed, I broke down in front of my mom, pleading for help. My mom asked my sister to assist, but only to guide me rather than do the work for me. My sister, skilled at projects, found it difficult not to take over, but she helped me navigate the process. This experience taught me that I needed to look beyond the reflection of my struggles and see the potential for growth and achievement.

Another vivid memory is from home economics. We had an assignment to bake a cake. Unfortunately, my mom had the flu that day. I told her I could manage it and would ask for help if needed. She directed me to the cake pans in the pull-out drawer under the stove. I took out what I thought was a cake pan and mixed my ingredients. When the cake was done, it looked more like a bus than a cake, so I decided to decorate it as a cake bus. I proudly presented it in the home economics room the next morning, but when it came time to grade, I received a zero. I was puzzled and thought the teacher must have missed a 1 and a 0.

When my mom heard about the grade, she came to school the next day to explain that her illness had prevented her from helping, but she felt my creativity deserved more than a zero. She argued that I had thought creatively about my cake bus, and the teacher agreed to adjust my grade to an eighty. I was relieved and pleased with the outcome. As my mom walked me to my next class, she said, "Well, now we know what a meatloaf pan is." I could not help but smile, grateful for my mom's support and understanding.

In a world obsessed with appearances, it is easy to fall into the trap of defining ourselves by the reflection we see in the mirror. For years the truth was, that I did not see beyond the reflection in the mirror for a long time. For years, the mirror was my go-to, the thing that defined me and my worth. I relied on it to measure who I was—through what I could see on the surface. It was not until later—much later—that I began to understand there was more to me than what stared back at me. The process of realizing this was not an overnight revelation; it was a slow, gradual journey that unfolded through different experiences in life. And even now, sometimes, the old story tries to creep back in, that familiar voice whispering the same old lie: "You're not smart enough."

For so long, I had allowed my looks to define me, to be the thing I relied on because it is what people always seemed to notice first. Compliments about my appearance came easily, and I leaned into that, believing that if I did not have beauty, I did not have much else. I became so accustomed to this narrative that when people began to seek me out for advice, it surprised me.

It was not about beauty or fashion. It was about life. Friends would come to me, sharing their problems, asking how I would manage demanding situations, or seeking encouragement when they felt stuck. At first, I was taken aback, unsure of why they were turning to me. I had grown so used to thinking of myself as someone only noticed for her looks that it felt foreign to be seen in a separate way. But with each conversation, I began to realize something—my value was not just tied to my appearance. I had something meaningful to offer beyond the surface: my thoughts, my kindness, my creativity. Slowly, I started to discover new parts of myself that had been overshadowed by the pressure to be perfect on the outside.

One of the most transformative periods in my life came during my time working at the gym. At first, it felt like people were drawn to me because of my appearance, but as I became more involved in my work, I noticed a shift. It was not just about how I looked anymore—it was about the value I brought to the table. I was no longer just the girl behind the desk or the pretty face greeting clients. I was designing personalized fitness programs, tailoring nutrition plans to suit individual needs, and walking people through their journeys toward better health. I became someone they could rely on not just for practical advice but for emotional support, motivation, and encouragement.

What surprised me the most was how much people trusted me with their struggles. They opened up to me about their insecurities, their health challenges, and their fears. And I realized that they were not seeking perfection from me—they were seeking guidance, someone who could listen, understand, and help them navigate their own transformations. It became clear that I was earning their trust through my expertise, my experience, and my genuine desire to see them succeed. My value was not tied to my looks anymore; it was in the connections I was building; in the way I was able to guide and inspire others through their struggles and victories. It was in those moments that I truly began to recognize my own strength, both as a professional and as a person.

I remember one client in particular, a woman who struggled with weight loss and body image issues. Initially, she came to me for practical advice about diet and exercise, but as time passed, I realized that what she really needed was not just a workout plan. She needed someone to listen to her fears, to understand her doubts, and to help her build confidence in herself. As I watched her transform—not just physically, but emotionally—I realized that my ability to connect with her, to help her see her own worth, had nothing to do with how I looked. It was about my capacity to inspire her, to lift her up, and to help her believe in herself. That was a powerful moment for me. It was a turning point where I began to understand that my value was not limited to what was on the outside.

When I became a hairstylist—another profession often associated with beauty—I found a deeper purpose in my work. Yes, there was satisfaction in helping people feel good about their appearance, in creating a beautiful hairstyle that gave someone confidence, but the real value lay in something more. My clients came to me not just for a haircut—they came for the connection created by our conversations, my listening ear, and the encouragement. I realized that my job was not just about physical transformation. It was about making people feel seen, heard, and valued. That is when I truly understood that my intelligence was not confined to books or tests. It was in the way I solved problems creatively, navigated challenges, and lifted others up. Intelligence, I realized, was not about know everything—it was about being compassionate, understanding people, and always being open to learning.

This slow evolution of understanding—that I was more than just my appearance—was transformative. It taught me that my worth did not come from how I looked, but from how I lived. My true strength, my true intelligence, lay in the way I treated others, in the way I supported and inspired them. It took years to fully embrace this, but with each step, I started to see myself more clearly. I began to value the parts of me that had nothing to do with beauty: my resilience, my ability to connect, my creativity. I stopped measuring my worth in the mirror and started measuring it by the impact I could have on others and the way I chose to show up in the world.

But that old story, the one that told me I was not smart enough, still tries to sneak back in from time to time. Even after all the growth I have experienced, even after learning to see my own worth, there are days when that story resurfaces. It is in moments of doubt—when I question my abilities, when I feel overwhelmed by a challenge, or when I wonder if people are still only seeing what is on the outside. That old narrative tries to pull me back, to make me believe that I am not enough; that the version of myself I once knew is all I will ever be.

I have also learned something crucial: that story is not the truth. It is just a story. A story I used to believe, a story I used to think defined me. But it does not anymore. I am not the girl who is only seen for her beauty. I am not the girl who believes she is not smart enough, not worthy enough, or not enough in any way. Those old beliefs are just that—old. They do not control me anymore, and they certainly do not get to shape my future.

When I think about that little girl staring at her reflection, I wish I could tell her what I know now: that intelligence is not measured by grades or test scores. It is found in resilience, in compassion, and in the way you choose to see the world and the people around you. It is in the courage to believe that you are more than what others perceive on the outside.

The reflection in the mirror will always be there, but it no longer defines me. I have learned to see beyond it, to embrace the parts of myself that I once thought was hidden or inadequate. I have discovered that I am enough, just as I am—not because of how I look, but because of who I am.

My love for mirrors started innocently enough. I remember, as a young girl, being fascinated by them. I would sit in front of my small compact mirror for hours, gazing at my reflection, perfecting my smile, checking my hair. At the time, I thought it was because I was vain—maybe a lot of people would have agreed. But as I have grown older, I realize now it was not about vanity. Mirrors were my way of searching for something deeper. When I looked in the mirror, I was not just seeing my face—I was searching for myself, trying to see the parts of me that were buried under the surface.

I have come to understand that mirrors are not just for checking your appearance. They are reflections of how you see yourself and what you believe about your worth. And there were so many times when I looked into that mirror and did not like what I saw, not because of my face, but because I did not believe in my own intelligence. I would sit there for hours, staring deep into my own eyes, thinking, I am not ugly, but I am dumb. I am not smart. So, I will have to fool people to accomplish things in life. Those were the thoughts that swirled in my mind for so long.

Looking back, I realize that many of the lessons I learned about myself were rooted in those moments of reflection. My mom often used mirrors as analogies when I was growing up. She would say, "When you are getting ready for a date, stand in front of the mirror, and ask yourself what you are going to allow on that date. Are you going to let him hold your hand? Will you let him kiss you?" She always emphasized that the mirror was a tool for self-reflection, for planning, for setting boundaries and sticking to them.

That advice stuck with me, and I have used it in so many areas of my life—not just on dates, but in job interviews, in friendships, in all my interactions. The mirror became a symbol of self-accountability. It helped me plan, to be mindful of what I would allow into my life. Every time I investigated it, I asked myself, what am I going to permit? What am I going to value about myself today?

I have mirrors everywhere in my life now. There is one in every room of my house, in my office, and even woven into the decorations I choose. But the truth is, it is no longer about my appearance. Each mirror has become a reflection of something much deeper, a symbol of self-awareness and accountability rather than vanity. These days, when I look into a mirror, I am not just checking my hair or seeing if my outfit looks good. I am asking myself questions that go far beyond the surface.

At night, when I stand at my bathroom sink brushing my teeth, I often find myself staring into the mirror, thinking about the day I have had. I ask myself, Am I proud of the person I was today? Did I live up to my own expectations, not just for what I accomplished but for how I treated others? Did I show kindness? Was I honest with myself and those around me? Did I stay true to my values, or did I let someone else's opinions sway me? These questions run through my mind as I stand there, staring into my own reflection.

Sometimes the answers are clear. Yes, I handled that difficult conversation well. Yes, I stood up for myself when I needed to. Yes, I took the time to be kind to someone who was struggling. Other nights, though, it is harder. I might catch a glimpse of myself and realize I have let stress or frustration get the best of me. I was not as patient as I could have been, or I allowed insecurity to creep back in, making me doubt my decisions.

The mirror has become a tool for self-reflection in the truest sense. It is a reminder that every day I have the opportunity to gain experience, to do better, and to be more aligned with the person I want to become. It is no longer just a reflection of my physical appearance; it is a reflection of my inner self, the person I am becoming through the choices I make and the actions I take.

In many ways, mirrors have become symbols of growth and accountability in my life. Each time I look at my reflection, I am not just seeing the face I present to the world—I am looking for the person I am striving to be. Am I living with integrity? Am I living up to the standards I have set for myself, or have I allowed myself to settle into old patterns of doubt and insecurity? The mirror forces me to confront these questions, to reflect not just on how I look but on how I live.

Over time, I have come to realize that this daily ritual of self-reflection has helped me grow in ways I never imagined. It has made me more mindful of the choices I make throughout the day, knowing that I will be asking myself those deeper questions later. I have become more intentional about how I spend my time and how I treat the people in my life. The mirror holds me accountable, not in a judgmental way but as a gentle reminder that I am constantly evolving.

I used to think that mirrors were tools for vanity, for making sure I looked good on the outside. Now I see that they are so much more than that. They have become windows into my soul, reflecting not just what I look like but who I am becoming. They remind me that growth is a process, that it is okay to have days where I stumble, but that it is important to keep moving forward, always striving to be a little better, a little truer to myself.

There were moments when I found myself staring in the mirror, focusing on my appearance, as if by doing so, I could avoid confronting the deeper emotions and insecurities I was trying to keep hidden. It was easier to fixate on the surface than to face the deeper questions about my worth, intelligence, and inner self.

On those nights when I stand at my bathroom sink, brushing my teeth and staring haltingly into the mirror, I find that most nights, I can answer my own question to self with a quiet, simple yes. I am proud of the person I am, not because I have reached some perfect version of myself, but because I am on the journey. I am learning, I am growing, and I am becoming more of the person I was always meant to be. The mirror does not define me—it just reflects the work I am doing, day by day, to live a life that feels honest and true.

When I look in the mirror and feel discomfort or dissatisfaction, it often goes beyond just physical appearance. The image staring back at me can sometimes reflect unresolved emotions, insecurities, or deeper issues I have been avoiding. It is easier for me to focus on the exterior—my looks, achievements, or roles in life—because delving into the heart and soul requires a vulnerability that can be uncomfortable, even painful.

We live in this world that often values outside appearance over individual substance, and this societal emphasis on just mere physical beauty can overshadow my personal journey of realizing that true worth comes from within our bodies and souls, and ultimately, from God's perspective. The scientific bias toward outward beauty often stubbornly impacts how I view true self. I do realize it is crucial to tie this sense of self and understanding to a deeper truth about my own identity and value.

When I only see the surface, I miss the fleeting opportunity to reflect on what is happening inside me. The image in the mirror might evoke on going discomfort. I found facing what lies beyond the reflection means confronting those fears we harbor, low self-esteem, past hurts, or unresolved pain. It is a defense mechanism to avoid looking deeper. Our heart holds the truth of who we are, and sometimes that truth can be challenging and difficult to face.

From a spiritual perspective, this process of looking inward can be guided by God's grace and understanding. My heart's struggles and insecurities are known to Him, and through faith, I can find the strength to confront them. My heart often reveals itself through my thoughts, emotions, and how I interact with myself and others. If the reflection in the mirror is challenging to embrace, it may be because I have not yet accepted or healed from those inner struggles. By seeking God's guidance, I can acknowledge the hidden parts of myself—the insecurities, failures, or moments of doubt—and understand that they do not define my worth but are part of my journey.

True transformation happens when I gather the courage to look past the surface and delve into my heart, acknowledging the deeper emotions, fears, and desires I have suppressed, with God's help. It is in this place of vulnerability, supported by divine love and grace, that I begin to heal, forgive myself, and grow. The mirror's reflection is just a starting point; the journey inward, with God's guidance, leads to the most significant and lasting change.

What do you think it takes for me to gather the courage to look beyond the surface and truly examine what is in my heart, with God's help?

In the end, the mirror has taught me that true beauty is not about perfection—it is about authenticity. It is about being willing to look at yourself honestly, flaws and all, and still choosing to show up every day with grace and determination. It is about accepting that while the reflection may change over time, the core of which I have remained, growing stronger with each step of the journey. And that, more than anything, is the kind of reflection I want to see looking back at me.

To reiterate our struggles with our own individual mirrors my story continues, as always in a world obsessed with appearances, it is easy to fall into that trap of defining ourselves by the reflection we see in the mirror. Again, for years I measured my internal worth by what people said about me, constantly seeking validation from the large and diverse outside world. My sister, with her effortless charm and intelligence, always seemed to attract admiration and praise. I, on the other hand, never ever received the kind of attention she did, which left me feeling extremely undervalued. Deep inside of me, I knew there was more to me than what met the all-seeing eye. I have always been more than just a pretty face.

My sister played a crucial role in supporting me with my schoolwork and deep personal struggles. She never made me feel inadequate, despite her knowing that I continuously struggled on a day-to-day basis. My sister's sweet encouragement and patience were unwavering to this day. She was always present in person or in spirit to explain concepts or to help me find solutions when I faced challenges. Whether it was those late-night study sessions or tackling difficult assignments together, she was a constant source of all around support, masterfully believing in my abilities even when I doubted myself. Her immense belief in me not only helped me academically but also instilled that elusive confidence that I could lovingly overcome any obstacle with the utmost perseverance and support. Through her unwavering guidance, I learned the immense value of encouragement in achieving academic success.

The enemy knew how to get to me, and it was never through my physical appearance—it was always in my head, challenging my intelligence and self-worth. I vividly remember a day in high school, sitting in a classroom full of my peers, nervously clutching my pencil as the teacher handed out a test. As I stared at the test, my mind went blank. The whispers of insecurity crept in, telling me I was not smart enough, that I would never measure up to my sister or anyone else. It felt like those voices were determined to convince me that my value was tied to my ability to perform perfectly in every situation. I'm happy to report those voices failed!

It took me countless years of mental and emotional work to peel back the layers of those lies and see myself for who I truly am. Slowly, I began to understand that my value is not confined to my looks or the fleeting approval of others. My mind is a treasure trove of ideas, creativity, and intelligence. I am capable of deep, critical thinking, solving complex problems, and engaging in thoughtful conversations. I am not a one-dimensional character in a book but a multifaceted individual with dreams, aspirations, and a relentless drive to make a difference.

Another important turning point in my journey came during a group project in college—a setting that always filled me with anxiety. I have always been hesitant to speak up, afraid that my ideas would not be good enough or that I would be dismissed. Surrounded by peers who seemed so sure of themselves, I often stayed silent, fearing judgment. This time, though, something was different. As we began discussing our approach to the project, I felt an exhilarating surge of confidence bubbling up within me. It was as if all the moments of doubt and insecurity were being challenged by a newfound belief in myself. I took a deep breath and decided to share my thoughts.

My voice trembled slightly as I started to speak, but I pushed through, outlining my ideas and vision for our project. To my surprise, instead of the dismissive looks or polite nods I expected, my classmates leaned in, genuinely engaged with what I was saying. They not only listened but also asked questions and offered constructive feedback, showing a level of respect and consideration that I had not anticipated. It was a revelation—an experience that felt like a light switch turning on, illuminating a path I had never fully seen before. I realized then that the value of my contributions was not based on perfection but on authenticity and perspective.

My ideas were unique because they came from my experiences and insights, and that made them worth sharing.

As this ongoing discussion continued, I grew more confident, while adding to the conversation with ease and enthusiasm. I was no longer a passive participant; I was actively shaping the direction of our project. That realization was transformative. It was not just about being heard; it was about recognizing that I had something valuable to contribute, that my voice and ideas mattered. For the first time, I saw myself as a capable and equal member of the group, not just someone trying to fit in or measure up to others. This experience marked a significant shift in how I viewed myself and my abilities. I started to believe that my thoughts, ideas, and insights had weight and significance and that my contributions could be effective. It was a small step, but it opened a world of possibilities for me, igniting a spark of self-confidence that would continue to grow and shape my journey.

My heart, too, adds to my worth. It beats with compassion, empathy, and kindness. I find joy in helping others, being a source of comfort and support. My capacity to love and be loved goes far beyond the superficial. It is in the relationships I build, the lives I touch, and the positive impact I strive to make in my community. I remember volunteering at a domestic violence shelter, where I met a young girl who reminded me so much of myself—unsure, seeking approval. I saw in her eyes the same fear I had felt for so long. We spent hours talking, and I shared my journey with her, hoping to offer a glimmer of hope. Seeing her smile and gain confidence over time reaffirmed that my worth was not just in my intellect but also in my ability to connect and uplift others.

This experience was a profound reminder of the transformative power of empathy and connection. As I continued volunteering, I found myself gravitating toward people who were in the same place I had been—lost, unsure, and in need of a little encouragement. Each conversation became an opportunity to offer not just words of comfort but a piece of myself. I listened to their stories with genuine interest, shared my own experiences, and, in doing so, we created a space where vulnerability was met with understanding, and pain was met with compassion.

When we talk about low self-esteem, the first thing that often comes to mind is the idea of not feeling pretty enough or not fitting into certain societal standards of beauty. But I am here to tell you that it is so much more than that. Recently, I did a podcast on self-worth titled "You Are Enough," and during the preparation for that episode, I had a powerful moment of self-reflection that really opened my eyes.

As Britt and I were studying and gathering our thoughts for the podcast, I realized something important. Just because I did not struggle with feeling ugly or unattractive did not mean that I did not have issues with self-worth and self-esteem. I had always thought that because I was not caught up in negative thoughts about my appearance, I was immune to the effects of low self-esteem. But as I delved deeper into the material we were preparing, something shifted inside me.

I started to remember moments when I felt stupid, moments when I felt like I was not smart enough or capable enough. These feelings of inadequacy began to surface, bringing back memories that I had buried deep within me. Memories of times when I questioned my intelligence, when I felt like I was an idiot, and when I allowed these negative thoughts to shape my perception of who I was. It was as if all those old wounds were reopening, and I was confronted with the reality that self-esteem is not just about how you look, but also about how you perceive yourself in every aspect of your life.

In that moment, I realized that I had been defining myself by the wrong standards. I had allowed those negative thoughts and memories to haunt me and dictate the kind of person I thought I was. But then, I remembered something crucial—I remembered what God says I am. I am not defined by those moments of doubt or by the harsh judgments I placed on myself. I am defined by what God says about me. He says that I am valuable, loved, and capable. He says that I am enough, just as I am.

This realization was incredibly freeing, and it gave me the strength to confront those negative thoughts head-on. I had to remind myself that my worth is not tied to my intelligence, my abilities, or even my appearance. My worth is found in Jesus, and through Him, I can find the confidence and peace that I had been searching for.

I want to encourage everyone who may be struggling with feelings of inadequacy or low self-esteem to find their worth in Jesus. He is the one who created you, who knows you intimately, and who loves you unconditionally. When you find your worth in Him, all those negative thoughts and self-doubts begin to lose their power. You start to see yourself through His eyes, and that is where true self-worth is found.

If you are feeling like you are not enough, if you are struggling with those old memories that try to drag you down, remember what God says about you. He says that you are fearfully and wonderfully made. He says that you are His masterpiece. And He will always make a way for you, even when it feels like there is no way forward. Trust in Him, and let His truth define who you are. You are enough, not because of what you do or how you look, but because of who you are in Him.

One moment that stands out is when the young girl, after weeks of meeting regularly, looked at me with a newfound spark in her eyes and said, "I think I can do this." It was a simple statement, but it carried the weight of newfound belief and courage. In that instant, I realized that my worth was not just something I needed to understand internally; it was something I could use to inspire others. The joy I felt from seeing her slowly blossom into someone who believed in her own potential was indescribable. It was as if I was watching a reflection of my own growth, reminding me that we all have the capacity to change, heal, and find our strength.

Every smile, every word of encouragement I offered, seemed to ripple outwards, creating waves of positive change not just in the shelter but within me as well. I learned that my heart had a unique role to play—a role that was not about grand gestures or world-changing feats, but about the small, meaningful connections that happen when you truly open yourself up to another person's experience. It is these moments of shared humanity that make life rich and fulfilling, and it is in these moments that I see my true worth. I am more than just a collection of thoughts and ideas; I am a conduit for love, a catalyst for hope, and a reminder that we all have the power to lift each other up.

I am resilient and strong, having faced challenges that tested my limits and emerged stronger. My scars tell stories of battles fought and won, of lessons learned and wisdom gained. They are a testament to my courage and determination—attributes that cannot be captured in a mere reflection. I remember the time I almost gave up on my dreams because I felt overwhelmed by the expectations placed on me. But each time I felt like quitting, I reminded myself of the challenges I had already overcome, the strength I had built, and the support system around me, especially my faith.

Recognizing my worth also means embracing my imperfections. They make me real, relatable, and uniquely me. I am a work in progress, constantly evolving and growing in God. My journey is not defined by how I look but by the steps I take, the choices I make, and the person I strive to become.

In moments of serious doubt, I remind myself consistently that my worth is solid and unshakeable. It is not whole fully granted by others' opinions or diminished by their wanton faultless criticisms. I am valuable simply because I am. I am a unique blend of intellect, emotion, spirit, and strength—a dynamic force with the potential and power to create, inspire, and transform.

When I look in the mirror now, I see more than just a reflection of my outward appearance. I see a person of profound substance and depth, someone who is not only proud of her lasting struggling journey but also excited for the bright future that lies ahead of me. The mirror in all it's unattainable glory no longer reveals just a conspicuous pretty face but instead reflects the unwavering essence of who I am—a remarkable individual with a true story that is uniquely my own, enriched with raw courage, growth, and unwavering devout faith.

I see and feel the deep strength that has carried me through those simple and difficult challenges, the resilience that has turned steadfast obstacles into opportunities, and the wisdom that has been cultivated through experiences both joyous and painful. This reflection is not confined to mere beauty; it is expansive and limitless, embracing the fullness of my individual character and the breadth and depth of my potential.

In this image, I recognize that my worth is not measured by external standards only by the richness of my inner self. I am more than the sum of my physical attributes; I am a testament to the power of perseverance, the strength of belief, and the beauty of a heart that has learned to love itself fully. I am SMART in every sense of the word, embodying the intelligence that comes from understanding and embracing my ultimate true value.

As I stand again before the mirror, I am reminded of my journey, my growth, and the incredible potential that lies within me. This reflection is a celebration of all that I have become and all that

I will continue to be. It is a powerful reminder that my worth is not confined to the surface but is a radiant, expansive truth that shines through every facet of my being.

As we come to the end of this journey together, I hope these pages have resonated with your own path. May you close this book with a profound sense of your boundless worth. Like me, you are a remarkable individual with a story rich in courage, growth, and an unshakable belief in your own values. You are more than that reflection in the mirror; you are the embodiment, radiant beacon of strength, wisdom, and limitless potential. Embrace this truth with all of your heart, continue to celebrate your unique journey, and let it guide you towards a future that shines as brightly as your own individual inner light. May you always walk forward with confidence and grace, knowing that your brilliance is both extraordinary and enduring.

About the Author

Janie E. Torbich of Ocean Isle Beach, NC, is an ambitious, loving, loyal, and overly motivated businesswoman. In a field dominated by men, Janie has stood out among her peers, rising to the rank of General Manager at a nationwide finance company based on the East Coast. Driven by her faith and the guidance of the Holy Spirit, Janie founded *Ladies in Transformation (L.I.T)*, a nonprofit organization dedicated to helping women strengthen their lives physically, spiritually, and emotionally. Through this platform, Janie has empowered countless women in active recovery, making a profound impact as a committed volunteer at CRCI's Rose House.

A devoted wife and proud mother of three—Joy, Riley, and Sadie—Janie is passionate about creating a world where everyone is respected and has access to equal education and employment opportunities. Her work reflects her belief in the transformative power of faith, resilience, and self-worth.

In *It's Not Always Smart to Be Pretty*, Janie shares her candid reflections on navigating the complexities of beauty, intelligence, and faith. With vulnerability and insight, she reveals the struggles and triumphs that have shaped her journey, encouraging readers to embrace their inner beauty and divine purpose.

A Message from the Author... "I pray that you will use this story of my life to stir up your inner beauty. No matter what life labels you, know that you were created as a child of God—worthy to be seen, heard, and loved."

www.ingramcontent.com/pod-product-compliance
Lightning Source LLC
Chambersburg PA
CBHW051159120626
46547CB00012B/1125